QUEER SOCIAL WORK

Mira Farrow

QUEER SOCIAL WORK

Cases for **LGBTQ+** Affirmative Practice

Edited by

TYLER M. ARGÜELLO

Columbia University Press   *New York*

Columbia University Press
Publishers Since 1893
New York   Chichester, West Sussex
cup.columbia.edu

Library of Congress Cataloging-in-Publication Data

Names: Argüello, Tyler M., author.
Title: Queer social work : cases for LGBTQ+ affirmative practice /
    Tyler Argüello.
Description: New York : Columbia University Press, 2019. | Includes
    bibliographical references and index.
Identifiers: LCCN 2019019486 | ISBN 9780231194006 (hardcover) |
    ISBN 9780231194013 (paperback) | ISBN 9780231550604 (ebook)
Subjects: LCSH: Sexual minorities—Social conditions. | Social
    work with sexual minorities.
Classification: LCC HQ73 .A74 2019 | DDC 306.76—dc23
LC record available at https://lccn.loc.gov/2019019486

Cover symbol: "Progress" Pride Flag by Daniel Quasar
(quasar.digital LLC), https://quasar.digital

Cover design: Lisa Hamm

To Lissa and the six-hour conversation
at thirty thousand feet that opened
Queer possibilities.

"Speaking nearby" (versus "speaking for") is one that . . . does not objectify, does not point to an object as if it is distant from the speaking subject or absent from a speaking place. A speaking that reflects on itself and comes very close to a subject without, however, seizing or claiming it. A speaking in brief, whose closures are only moments of transition opening up to other possible moments of transition. . . . It is an attitude in life, a way of positioning oneself in relation to the world.

—Trinh T. Minh-ha

CONTENTS

A NOTE ON LANGUAGE

Coming to Terms

"QUEER"

The term "LGBTQ+" is partial and insufficient; nevertheless, it is used throughout this text as it seeks to encompass the ever-evolving communication around sexualities and genders, inclusive of lesbian, gay, bisexual, transgender, queer, questioning, asexual, intersex, two-spirit, genderqueer, pansexual, and beyond. Interchangeably but at times parallel, the contested term "Queer" is deployed as a critically informed, necessarily unstable term that complicates dominantly defined categories, such as gay. Queer accommodates diversity within identities and pays attention to social and material forces—especially normativizing forces, such as race/class/gender/beyond, cultural practices, and lived contexts—that constrain and inform sexualities and genders beyond discreet behaviors or nominal identitarian-based categories. Queer in this case finds much animation from the theoretical and material lineage of Queer theory; for a fuller discussion, see Argüello (2016), Hall et al. (2013), Jagose (1996), Sullivan (2003), and Yep (2003). That said, it is important to recognize in this imperative rhetorical maneuver that Queer has had a long-standing sociohistorical trajectory. Queer, akin to homosexual, gay, or lesbian, among others, has a mixed history of being a principal term of abuse against LGBTQ+ people denoting and/or evoking particular eras in the development of LGBTQ+ identities—as well as being a chosen term by LGBTQ+ people to self-identify, reclaim, and/or to describe sub-/cultures and behaviors. Still today, the term "Queer" can evoke strong reactions from within and outside LGBTQ+ communities. For a fuller discussion about the sociohistorical context of Queer, see Alexander et al. (2018), Chauncey (1994), Dynes (1990), and Jagose (1996).

HIV, PREP, PEP, TASP, U=U

Whether or not someone is infected, HIV is already inside all of us. This is to say, HIV/AIDS has been one of the most profound public health crises of modern times—let alone a persistent breathtaking exemplar of intersectional social *in*justice. Even more, it has been an individual through community-wide traumatizing experience, in particular for LGBTQ+ people. Its intergenerational effects are barely beginning to be manifest, understood, and acknowledged. The virus has touched everyone's life—whether through infection, chronic anxieties, public health messaging, severe loss and grief, sexual health education, screening and testing, various risk factors, a chronic silent presence, or, among other ways, through the structural mechanisms that fortify its continued transmission and proliferation. In fact, today, some may remark that HIV does not figure into their day-to-day life or it is simply not a worry; possibly a sign of the fragile privilege for some that has been mounted over the years of fighting the epidemic and making advances, both ideologically and in terms of interventions.

As in the early days of AIDS, social work has a pivotal role in the prevention and care of people living with HIV, as well as those individuals and communities at risk. Since those early days, there have been substantive advances in HIV care and prevention; unfortunately, on the whole, the training of social workers has trailed in staying abreast of such knowledge and technologies. In conducting affirmative work with *any and all* LGBTQ+ people nowadays and in the future, discussions must include attention to sexual health and well-being, including dialogue about HIV prevention and care. This can certainly start during the initial biopsychosocial assessment when working with new clients, or this can become part of the archive of questions, knowledge, and psychoeducation that a clinician brings into the proverbial room with both new and existing clients.

Even more, this work must address advances in prevention and care—in particular PrEP, TasP, and U=U (Centers for Disease Control and Prevention, 2015, 2018, 2019). The HIV drug "cocktail" or Antiretroviral Therapy (ART) was introduced in 1996, to treat the infection in people diagnosed with HIV. Since 1998, a combination of those medications has been used as a protocol called PEP (post-exposure prophylaxis), for when an HIV-negative person takes antiretroviral medications to prevent infection after being potentially exposed to the HIV virus. In 2011, the Centers for Disease Control and Prevention (CDC) announced standards of care and prevention called TasP, referring to Treatment as Prevention. Decidedly, the CDC recommends that people who live with HIV can best care for their health by maintaining an undetectable viral load by taking ART. An additional benefit of reducing the amount of virus in the body is that it helps prevent transmission to others via sexual contact or sharing syringes; this is called "treatment as prevention."

In 2012, the CDC provided a new guideline for HIV prevention: Preexposure Prophylaxis, or PrEP. This is an antiretroviral medication, or one "little blue pill," taken daily by people (regardless of sexual orientation or gender) who are HIV-negative, which can be used to prevent acquiring HIV. Daily PrEP can reduce the risk of getting HIV from sex by more than 90 percent, and by more than 70 percent for those who inject drugs. PrEP is indicated for any HIV-negative person who is at increased risk for HIV. While awareness and use of PrEP has increased each year since 2012, there is still a long way to go. Some of the biggest barriers to PrEP getting to those most at-risk who could benefit greatly from its use, as well as the public more generally, include the fact that only one in three prescribing providers knows about PrEP along with the enduring problems of homophobia, stigma, and discrimination. It should be noted that any provider with prescriptive authority can prescribe PrEP (Centers for Disease Control and Prevention, 2015; pleasePrEPme.org, 2018).

Finally, following these guidelines, in 2016, a prevention campaign was launched called U=U, signaling that undetectable equals untransmissible. The campaign is reinforcing the consensus by the World Health Organization, the CDC, and more than 750 other organizations worldwide that people whose HIV viral load is stably suppressed cannot transmit the virus. To that end, this campaign directs attention to equal access to HIV prevention and to technologies based on science, not stigma.

For more information about PrEP and these other issues, please utilize the following empirical resources:

CDC information and guidelines on HIV, care, and prevention
www.cdc.gov/hiv/
Find a PrEP provider and training resources
www.pleaseprepme.org

U=U campaign

www.preventionaccess.org

Visualizing HIV, PrEP

aidsvu.org

REFERENCES

Alexander, J., Meem, D. T., & Gibson, M. A. (2018). *Finding out: An introduction to LGBTQ studies* (3rd ed.). Thousand Oaks, CA: Sage.

Argüello, T. M. (2016). Fetishizing the health sciences: Queer theory as a social work intervention. *Journal of Gay & Lesbian Social Services, 28*(3), 1–14.

Centers for Disease Control and Prevention. (2015). Daily pill can prevent HIV: Reaching people who could benefit from PrEP. Retrieved from https://www.cdc.gov/vitalsigns/hivprep/

Centers for Disease Control and Prevention (2018). HIV treatment as prevention. Retrieved from https://www.cdc.gov/hiv/risk/art/index.html

Centers for Disease Control and Prevention. (2019). PrEP. Retrieved from https://www.cdc.gov/hiv/basics/prep.html

Chauncey, G. (1994). *Gay New York: Gender, urban culture, and the making of the gay male world, 1890–1940.* New York, NY: Basic Books.

Dynes, W. R. (1990). *Encyclopedia of homosexuality.* New York, NY: Garland.

Hall, D. E., Jagose, A., Bebell, A., & Potter, S. (2013). *The Routledge queer studies reader.* New York, NY: Routledge.

Jagose, A. (1996). *Queer theory: An introduction.* New York, NY: New York University Press.

pleasePrEPme.org. (2018). Helping people access pre-exposure prophylaxis: A frontline provider manual on PrEP research, care and navigation [PDF]. Retrieved from https://www.pleaseprepme.org/prepnavigatormanual

Sullivan, N. (2003). *A critical introduction to queer theory.* New York, NY: New York University Press.

Yep, G. A. (2003). The violence of heteronormativity in communication studies: Notes on injury, healing, and queer world-making. *Journal of Homosexuality, 45*(2–4), 11–59.

INTRODUCTION

There is a poverty of language when it comes to LGBTQ+ people and cultures. Since the beginning of my own pathway to become a Queer social work scholar, professor, and practitioner—and over my lifetime as a Queer person and citizen subject—matters of sexuality and gender have too often been relegated to nominal variables, two-dimensional demographics, sources for problem-oriented reasoning, risk moderators, sources of trauma and injustice, romanticized notions of clients or friends, or sequestered existences at work and in other spaces. Implicitly and explicitly, matters of sexuality and gender have been approached with abject prejudice, stigmas, phobias, and pathologizing discourses. The net result, for me as a social work professional, has been the sense that, by and large, this world hopes that Queer people do not exist. I am not the only person who still has this sort of lived experience.

It is not all doom and gloom, however. One of the great resiliencies of LGBTQ+ people and cultures is their critical relationship with language and communication. LGBTQ+ people can be understood as *counterpublics* (cf. Warner, 2002), marginalized people whose lived experiences involve shuttling between an oppressive world and their ground-up practices of reclamation and resistance. From that perspective, Queer identities serve a strategic function: they mediate between one's marginalized lived experience and the larger culture of invalidation and injustice. Key to this is the language created and contorted by Queer people to describe themselves and their lives. As such, the experiences of Queer folks become inscribed into their communicative practices that articulate their found, claimed, and performative identities. These articulations effectively give life to Queer people—and more critically describe what has too often been unavailable and nullified because of the impotency of normative language to fully appreciate sexualities and genders. Normative language and normative ideologies are insufficient to provide meaning to sexualities and genders, and typically they inadequately afford the operative space to explore them and the intersections therein. In this sense, LGBTQ+ identities are not simply nouns that start to cohere experiences—they also function as verbs, that is, a way of active questioning, a continual process of becoming and breathing life into Queer possibilities.

In the grandest sense, tending to Queer identities and making manifest these lived realities is a world-making project. This is where social work steps in. Social workers can support, advocate for, and intervene. Our technologies of confronting injustice, amplifying change initiatives, and leveraging hope provide the space for differences to exist, to find footing in the world, and ultimately to thrive. In particular, social work programs are mandated to provide an educational culture that is inclusive and affirmative of LGBTQ+ people and cultures (CSWE, 2015). The profession is committed to support diversity, promote social justice, and challenge oppression (NASW, 2017). Despite this commitment, I have found over time as a student, practitioner, researcher, and educator that a Queer-affirmative approach can be elusive in practice. It is common to hear students and colleagues say something to the effect of, "Yes, but what does LGBTQ+ affirmative work look like? How do you do *that?*" After all, LGBTQ+ affirmative work is distinct from merely saying that you are an ally to LGBTQ+ people. Even more confounding, there is no singular way to do affirmative work. Applied practice styles are as varied as the identities and behaviors of Queer people themselves.

The case studies that comprise this book evidence contemporary LGBTQ+ identities and explore ways to approach the active negotiation of meaning making and behavior change, for both the client and the social worker. In these case studies, LGBTQ+ and Queer are both noun and verb, simultaneously about naming *and* creating a world in which to exist. In social work curriculum today, it is common to either not cover LGBTQ+ affirmative practice or to rely on panels of LGBTQ+ people, which fosters exoticization and places the burden on Queer people to speak for their communities. In contrast, these cases highlight current client situations of Queer people and empirically grounded LGBTQ+ affirmative work. Rather than leaving the case study inert on the table in the classroom, this collection shows pathways, grounded strategies, voices, and experiences of Queer people, both clients and social workers.

There are some textbooks for social work students on practice with LGBTQ+ people and communities. This collection of case studies does not try to supplant them. Rather, it can work in tandem—but may more effectively bring to life Queer experiences, practitioner conundrums, best practices, and examples of how all this can play out in the messy day-to-day world of practice. In that sense, this text is not a collection of moments of closure or the final word from experts on what must be done. Instead, these case studies are moments of opening in the style of Trinh T. Minh-ha, a "speaking nearby" that approximates Queer clients and social workers and brings the reader to a point of departure, not one of certainty. This text is a jumping-off point for self-reflection, for opening up possibilities, and for producing a space that allows Queerness to exist. It is pedagogical in practice and emancipatory in intent. It works, in part, to redress the poverty of LGBTQ+ language and cultures in social work training and practice. And, it decidedly shows how anti-LGBTQ+ stigmas and oppression hurt Queer people, all the while seeking an affirmative and critical praxis.

QUEER-AFFIRMATIVE PRACTICE

Queer-affirmative work begins with both an immersion into new knowledge archives and a deep dive into the hard work of self-reflection. Working as an ally (typically as an outsider) with a marginalized community is a hallmark of social work. Social workers' training and their ongoing practice must be geared toward cultural competence and social justice for LGBTQ+ communities, as well as other marginalized groups (CSWE, 2015; NASW, 2017). At face value and pragmatically, cultural competence means building relationships and trust with client systems, consciously tending to the ways in which knowledge is developed, using dynamic assessments, and deploying interventions consistent with the client system's worldview. Cultural competence is not voyeurism, fetishizing the (Queer) Other, nor is it simply an intellectual endeavor. Rather, it involves active engagement with one's self and the environment in which one lives, as well as cultivating knowledge, awareness, and exposure. That is, cultural competence is experiential and unending, appreciating the person-in-environment (Adams & Bell, 2016; Adams et al., 2018). A culturally competent approach involves understanding how oppression, power, and privilege affect, operate through, and become reproduced by individuals, groups, and structures. It takes into account how vulnerable populations lack power and privilege and how, in turn, they are marginalized, disenfranchised, and subject to inequities. This process requires that social workers increase insight into their own stigmas, biases, complicity, and participation in oppressive behaviors and structures—and it calls for engagement in allied behaviors working for social justice, equity, and empowerment. What is more, the burden of culturally competent work is not for the Other, e.g., LGBTQ+ person or community, to educate the social work student or professional. It is the ethical imperative, moral mandate, and professional obligation of social workers to continually train themselves in service of increasing cultural competence and responsiveness.

The task does not end with cultural competence. Competence around Queer matters and communities must be partnered with an affirmative standpoint and practice. (To be clear, both the Council on Social Work Education [CSWE] and the National Association of Social Workers [NASW] have published documents that oppose and condemn conversion and reparative therapies or sexual orientation change efforts [CSWE, 2016; NASW, 2015; NASW National Committee on Lesbian, Gay, and Bisexual Issues, 2000].) Generally, LGBTQ+ affirmative interventions involve an explicit validation of Queer identities, inclusive of an appreciation for the diversity of identities along the spectrum of sexualities and genders (Alessi, 2014; Craig, Austin, & Alessi, 2013; Crisp & McCave, 2007; Pachankis, 2014); the starting point for this undoubtedly begins in the social work classroom setting and curriculum (Wagaman, Shelton, & Carter, 2018). LGBTQ+ affirmative care recognizes that Queer people live with chronic stress and experience the social and health inequities that result from existing in an oppressive, discriminatory, and phobic society. So interventions with Queer people and communities must tend to these domains, and social workers must be accountable to their clients; they must continually assess their own attitudes and beliefs and commit themselves to action to reduce stigma and discrimination.

We know that heterosexist attitudes among practitioners can reduce their empathy for LGBTQ+ people and even harm them (Love, Smith, Lyall, Mullins, & Cohn, 2015). Like the general population, social workers can and do often have subtle (though sometimes active) phobias and practices toward Queer people that are left unexamined and therefore appear in their practice. These prejudices, coupled with low knowledge and self-awareness, create poor service delivery, misdiagnosis, pathologizing, and deprecation (Love et al., 2015). In turn, Queer people's experience of this sort of *non*affirmative practice can result in dissatisfaction with services, avoiding care, or omitting critical information.

Vital to this Queer-affirmative work is formulating the case from a competent and critical standpoint. Case formulation, in general, is an essential part of any clinical work; this core skill is typically the bridge between assessment and intervention (Eells, 2015). Whereas applied disciplines and clinical traditions can have a singular approach to formulation, this text provides a more general and integrative model for conducting LGBTQ+ affirmative case formulation. Each contributor provides their own voice, theoretical approach, clinical style, and recordkeeping practice and harnesses extant literature in their own way as they manifest a Queer-affirmative formulation to social work practice.

Sexualities and gender identities and expressions are not simply demographic variables to validate, affirm, and embed within the assessment—rather, they are squarely grounded starting points and the leitmotif of clinical work. The contributors foreground intersectional and LGBTQ+ concepts and practices at every turn. In this way, this text is theoretically driven and integrated, presenting multiple levels of theory, often with a critical and constructionist edge. The work throughout this text is also evidence based in multiple ways. The cases are empirically driven by contemporary lived experiences of client systems, social work professionals, and scholars. The conceptual and material approaches are grounded in existing interdisciplinary literature. And the animation for this varied work is driven by available knowledge about LGBTQ+ social and health inequities (Bostwick, Boyd, Hughes, & West, 2014; IOM, 2011; U.S. Department of Health and Human Services, 2014).

Finally, this book is generalizable. Although not *statistically* generalizable to the entire population of LGBTQ+ people or social workers, it does offer *analytic* generalizability and transferability among its cases. With this, we contribute empirically based knowledge to the larger body of a continually developing theoretical domain for Queer-affirmative case formulation and care (Polit & Beck, 2010). This is to say that these case studies do not tell the reader a single way to think or do the work, nor do they lay some colonizing claim to absolute knowledge or authority. Instead, these case studies provide a space for this work to exist, for the potential for a critical and Queer edge to live in practice, and for the possibility of what can be known and done when affirmation and validation are extended to the LGBTQ+ client system and the social worker.

THE FIELD OF SOCIAL WORK AND LGBTQ+ AFFIRMATIVE PRACTICE

As social workers, we attend to integration across field work, courses, and competencies. But this integration can be poorly sustained or even absent when it comes to LGBTQ+ communities and their inequities. This collection of Queer case studies emerged from the work of the Council on Sexual Orientation and Gender Identity and Expression (CSOGIE), one of the diversity councils of the CSWE. My Queer colleagues on this council and across my career have something in common: we are concerned about comprehensive, accessible, pragmatic, and integrative pedagogical materials that evince cases of contemporary lived experiences of LGBTQ+ people.

Social work is catching up. In recent years, much original research has been published that illuminates the strengths, deficiencies, and perceived biases in LGBTQ+ content in social work programs (Craig, Dentato, Messinger, & McInroy, 2016; Craig, McInroy, Dentato, Austin, & Messinger, 2015; Dentato, Craig, Messinger, Lloyd, & McInroy, 2014; Dentato et al., 2016; Gezinski, 2009; Hicks & Jeyasingham, 2016; Martin et al., 2009; McPhail, 2004; Papadaki, 2016). This archive speaks to a paucity of LGBTQ+ material in social work courses, a dissatisfaction with training and preparation for practice, a failure to assess student competency around LGBTQ+ issues, a tepid classroom culture, too few LGBTQ+ field placements, and an expressed need for cultural responsiveness and critical self-interrogation around Queer issues by social work students and faculty. There is a body of literature that interrogates the interpersonal relationships among social work students and LGBTQ+ faculty and *between* heterosexual and LGBTQ+ faculty, including investigating forms of discrimination, microaggressions, and nullification. This body of literature shows chronic invalidations, systemic heteronormativity, disruption of the learning environment, erasure of LGBTQ+ content in social work history, hostility toward Queer faculty, abject phobia, and damage to overall well-being (Dentato et al., 2016; Johnson, 2014; Messenger, 2009; Turner, Pelts, & Thompson, 2018). Finally, there is research and practice by social work scholars that responds and works to redress these trends. In particular, CSOGIE has produced LGBTQ+ affirmative best-practice standards for accredited social work programs. The recent *Rainbow Papers* translate both the implicit and explicit curriculum for social work programs to craft a comprehensive Queer-affirmative environment for learning (Austin et al., 2016; Craig et al., 2016). And recent edited volumes on social work practice with LGBTQ+ communities (Dentato, 2017; Hillcock & Mulé, 2017; Mallon, 2017) provide a wide-ranging review of literature and best practices, steeped in affirmative approaches.

This text is a furthering of these efforts. As I often tell my students, there is no way through the fire except *through* the fire. To do the work requires that you do the work. This text has been a work in progress, driven by my commitment to better serve LGBTQ+ people, my social work students, supervisees, and faculty colleagues. Very importantly, this text circles back to the perennial question from students and practitioners, "Yes, but what does Queer-affirmative practice actually look like?" On the whole, it aims to bridge the divide between social workers and the Queer people and issues they study (cf. Brown, 1995). This book works to facilitate connections between social work students, educators, professionals, and organizations on the one hand and their own local Queer communities and constituents on the other. And it does this through pragmatic integration of lived experiences, ethics, applied standards, and best practices.

It seeks to offer concrete, comparative case formulations that manifest culturally responsive and contemporary LGBTQ+ practice. This project is not simply a prompt for classroom discussion or a clinical snapshot devoid of context. Instead, these cases are a progressive pedagogical tool. They can be—and are designed to be—triangulated with student inquiry and development, educator expertise, critical thinking, companion texts, and emerging literature. In that way, they evidence integration, manifest social work competencies, and provide a forum for the often-unvoiced stories of marginalized communities and the practitioners who serve them.

Some social work programs incorporate explicit elective LGBTQ+ courses, but this text does not serve only those curricular ends. While matters of sexuality and gender frame and formulate these cases, these client systems and their situations also evince complicated and contested existences of people who live on the margins of American society. The cases in this book bring forward ethical issues and problems endemic to multilevel social work practice. Even more, the standpoint of each of the authors illuminates situations in which social justice and intersectional analysis are predominant in applied work. The ideal social work student reader or social work instructor using this text is one who seeks to embody the tripartite social worker—a scholar, practitioner, and activist. This text can, for example, be used in advanced clinical practice classes to deconstruct problems and processes in behavioral health practice. At the same time, given the aim for increasing competence, students in many other social work courses can read these cases to examine their own insights, reflections, stigmas, and biases. Shuttling between these ends, readers can use this text on the basis of demographics, as they will find a variety of social issues, clinical problems, and LGBTQ+ identities within.

Students and instructors could also harness this text along-side another textbook that more broadly surveys the state of knowledge around LGBTQ+ people. Texts on LGBTQ+ or Queer studies can be critical adjunctive resources to broaden the theoretical exposure and terrain of this work. And, obviously, these cases can be used alongside general social work practice methods textbooks to illuminate just what it looks like to conduct Queer-affirmative social work practice.

THE TEXT

When writing this book, we sought to incorporate unity, differences, and tensions. This is a way to speak back to the diversity of client systems, social problems, and professional practice styles. There is no single way to do applied work or to have LGBTQ+ lived experiences, so this book never suggests that Queer-affirmative work can look only one way or is arrived at by simply plugging variables into some calculus for Queer-affirmative social work. Instead, the vignettes offer trenchant examples of the clients who walk through the doors for help every day.

The contributing authors are social work scholars, educators, and practitioners who have diverse sexualities, genders, and intersectional identities. They have a wide array of multilevel experience in conducting social work practice, and these cases come from their experiences in the field. Because of this, the cases are necessarily imbued with the voices of their client system and the contributor's particular standpoint and, necessarily, the information about clients is anonymized if not also synergized across multiple clients. Given all the illustrated lived experiences and professional approaches, remember that each of these case studies is the work of authors seeking to give voice to otherwise marginalized and often *invisibilized* Queer people; this is to say, each case study opens space for the LGBTQ+ individuals, communities, and practitioners who are too often made silent and invisible through normative social work curriculum and practice. It goes without saying that this collection is not exhaustive. It does not cover the depth and breadth of all the issues in contemporary LGBTQ+ existences. Nor are all Queer peoples covered under the expansive rainbow alphabet umbrella. The authors recognize that there are many other ways to conceptualize and approach the work, and they acknowledge that the work is a process and perpetually in progress. In fact, the authors encourage more generative thinking and conversations among colleagues and students.

In the following pages, we will survey fourteen case studies. The reader should quickly take note that each study is neither overly elaborate nor overly abbreviated. This is intentional and strategic. One of the key skills any social worker can hone is how to come to the proverbial interdisciplinary table, either to offer a case to colleagues or to present a case in search of consult. To do this well, a social worker must reserve space for the client's story, be economical with words, be culturally responsive in approach, and be rigorous in analysis. Each of the contributors was offered a general framework for how to pattern out the case presentation, but they were also asked to compose the case consistent with their own voice, work style, and record-keeping norms. They could have written more about the case's background, formulation, and action plan, but that would have gone against the motivation to generate learning and discussion for the reader, as well as the Queer insistence on increasing tensions and possibilities.

While each case has different details, the reader will encounter a consistent pattern to how they unfold. The overview of case studies that follows this section details the primary operating LGBTQ+ and intersecting identities of the client/system; the primary mental/health and psychosocial issues at hand; the level of practice (i.e., micro, mezzo, macro); the most salient Educational Policy and Accreditation Standards, or EPAS (CSWE, 2015); and the relevant ethical codes (NASW, 2017). In addition, the overview provides an indication of the nature of practice for the social worker, that is, "generalist" (e.g., pre-MSW or MSW student); "MSW" (e.g., a newly minted graduate or pre-licensed social worker); "Post-MSW" (e.g., a seasoned social worker); or "Advanced Clinical" (e.g., a licensed social worker, typically focused on micro-level practice).

Following this overview, there is a collection of questions that are generally applicable to all the case studies. From there, the reader moves into the case studies. Each case is presented in two parts to illustrate the topics and perspectives you will encounter when conducting contemporary social work with LGBTQ+ individuals and communities. Part one of each case study presents the case itself and localized guiding questions in order to facilitate educational discussions and elicit critical thinking. Part two of each case presents the comparative case formulations, treatment and action plans, and references and resources.

Part One

- *Case Study*: A vignette of an individual, group, organizational, or community practice, manifesting intersectional identities, kinship systems, and pertinent factors of age, geography, health, and mental health.
- *Guiding Questions*: A series of questions to prompt discussion about issues for supervision and professional development.

Part Two

- *Case Formulation*: Each contributor provides both a "generalist" formulation and a "culturally responsive and Queer-affirmative" formulation to manifest application of theory and practice expertise to make sense of the case in a LGBTQ+ affirmative manner.
- *Treatment and Action Planning*: A plan that discusses and prioritizes areas of intervention and strategies for dealing with the issues at hand and promoting recovery, well-being, and an LGBTQ+ affirmative path forward.
- *References and Resources*: The cited references are listed along with other resources relevant to the case.

How should the reader approach this text? One approach is to begin with the vignette itself, detached from the guiding questions, case formulation, plan, and references. Each case can be approached through the lens of the universal questions. Students could also read through the case and articulate how they would deconstruct it through their own formulation, treatment, action plan, and resources or references. In this approach, students should engage with issues of power, privilege, and oppression operating within the case and within themselves. From the perspective of increasing cultural competence and critical consciousness, through self-reflection and guided discussion, readers can tap into automatic reactions and socialized biases. Quite commonly when encountering Queer issues, both insiders and outsiders to the community may have reactions of disgust, fetishization, sensationalism, pity, romanticizing, abject dismissal, or invalidation. Whatever the situation for readers, they must recognize these reactions and transform them in service of their professional duties, clinical development, and effective practice.

A second approach is to pair a case study with a given week's lecture or seminar in a practice course, an LGBTQ+ elective, a course on human behavior and the social environment, or another compatible course. The chapters could be used in a case study method or as a culminating example toward the latter part of class. In this way, the vignette and the case-specific questions can prompt the students to analyze, apply other practice content, and try out an LGBTQ+ affirmative response. Students can engage with a general assessment framework to locate salient information about the case. One common foundational assessment framework is biopsychosocial (Hutchinson, 2014). Within that perspective, student readers can have some analytic guideposts when sifting through the complicated and contested situation of each case study. They can take notes about the biological (physiology, growth, development), psychological (relationships, perception, emotional reactions, self-concept, attitudes and behaviors about sex), and social or cultural (influences, intersectional identities, sexual personhood, sexual and gender health, histories) dimensions of the case, as well as other pertinent information (socioeconomics, education, religiosity, spirituality, media exposure, socializations). After their initial assessment and discussion of part one, the instructor can provide part two of the case for a comparative analysis with the work just done by the students.

A third approach is using this text as a starting point for companion work. While students (and faculty) should seek the reflection, knowledge, and skill building laid out throughout this introduction, these cases are places from which to expand the repertoire of the social work student. That is, after moving through some or all the case studies, students can engage in a self-reflection journaling assignment. While journaling is common to most any practice course, in this case I suggest a journaling practice that does not have to pertain to goings-on in the field or other work with clients. In service of developing critical consciousness, students may engage in a deep analysis of their own internalized or socialized cisheterosexism, monoheteronormativity, homonormativity, and other intersecting biases. This text would work well with a related elective course, helping to create sustained space and time over a semester to revisit and interrogate students' own prejudices. On the other hand, students could be asked to use the structure and analytic framework of these cases to write up their own case studies of client systems with whom they are working, especially those who are LGBTQ+. However, a Queer-affirmative framework is not limited to LGBTQ+ clients. In fact, the Queer-affirmative framework provided in this book may be generative and, dare we say, emancipatory for non-LGBTQ+ client systems. The specialty of a Queer-affirmative approach is to ardently interrogate normative structures and practices. And that applies to everyone.

No matter which of these three approaches readers of this text may take, there are overall learning objectives. After working through this collection of cases, readers should be able to describe an LGBTQ+ affirmative approach to conducting multilevel social work practice. This includes formulating cases generally and particularly in a way that affirms Queer lives. Pragmatically, the reader should be aware of contemporary intersectional issues involved in the welfare and care of LGBTQ+ clients, including material resources for further professional development and avenues for prospective referrals or other brokering. More sensitively, readers should engage in critical self-reflection, a way of increasing their cultural competence. Finally, working through this collection should provide the reader with a more robust ethic of cultural humility, a greater sense of curiosity, and an allied standpoint in working with LGBTQ+ client systems.

I recommend that readers practice "speaking nearby" as well as "*standing* nearby," by which I mean bearing witness to Queer stories of pain, resilience, survival, and pride. This "nearby" sensibility gives us a point of departure, an opening up of possibility—and, perhaps most critically, it creates space in the world for LGBTQ+ people to exist.

It is with a strident commitment to socially just, Queer-affirmative work that the contributors and I offer these case studies to fellow social work students, faculty, and professionals.

OVERVIEW OF CASE STUDIES

Case Study	*The "Addict"*
Primary Operating LGBTQ+ Identities	Cisgender gay male
Primary Operating Intersecting Identities	White, Episcopalian, widower
Mental/Health or Psychosocial Issues	Aging, HIV+, substances, trauma, grief/loss
Level of Practice	Micro, mezzo
Nature of Practice	Post-MSW, Advanced Clinical
2015 EPAS	2, 3, 4, 7, 8, 9
2017 NASW Ethics	1.01—Commitment to clients
	1.05—Cultural awareness and social diversity
	2.03—Interdisciplinary collaboration
	2.09—Incompetence of colleagues

2.10—Unethical conduct of
colleagues

3.08—Continuing education
and staff development

4.02—Discrimination

5.01—Integrity of the profession

Case Study	*Employee Assistance Program*
Primary Operating LGBTQ+ Identities	Cisgender female, polyamorous
Primary Operating Intersecting Identities	African American
Mental/Health or Psychosocial Issues	Depressive symptoms, career stress, microaggressions
Level of Practice	Micro
Nature of Practice	Post- / MSW
2015 EPAS	1, 2, 6, 7
2017 NASW Ethics	1.01—Commitment to clients
	1.05 (a–c)—Cultural awareness and social diversity
	4.01 (a–c)—Competence
	5.02 (c)—Evaluation and research

Case Study	*Trans-itioning, Again*
Primary Operating LGBTQ+ Identities	Trans masculine, gay man
Primary Operating Intersecting Identities	African American, HIV+, professional
Mental/Health or Psychosocial Issues	Anxiety, post-trans health care, middle age, sexual behaviors, STIs, intimacy

Level of Practice   Micro, mezzo

Level of Practice	Micro, mezzo
Nature of Practice	Advanced Clinical
2015 EPAS	1, 2, 3, 4, 6, 7, 8, 9
2017 NASW Ethics	1.01—Commitment to clients
	1.05—Cultural awareness and social diversity
	2.03—Interdisciplinary collaboration
	2.09—Incompetence of colleagues
	3.01—Supervision and consultation
	3.08—Continuing education and staff development
	5.01—Integrity of the profession

Case Study	*Trying to Conceive*
Primary Operating LGBTQ+ Identities	Lesbian
Primary Operating Intersecting Identities	Married, white, culturally Jewish, adult, socioeconomically advantaged, parent, mother
Mental/Health or Psychosocial Issues	Adjustment disorder, rule out dysthymia and anxiety
Level of Practice	Micro, mezzo
Nature of Practice	Advanced clinical
2015 EPAS	1, 2, 4, 6, 7, 8, 9
2017 NASW Ethics	1.01—Commitment to clients
	1.02—Self-determination
	1.04—Competence

1.05—Cultural awareness and
social diversity

1.16—Referral for services

2.03—Interdisciplinary
collaboration

3.02—Education and training

4.02—Discrimination

5.01—Integrity of the profession

Case Study	*The Colleague*
Primary Operating LGBTQ+ Identities	Transgender male
Primary Operating Intersecting Identities	Young adult, Jewish
Mental/Health or Psychosocial Issues	Rural, transitioning, transphobia, workplace discrimination
Level of Practice	Mezzo
Nature of Practice	Generalist
2015 EPAS	1, 2, 3, 5
2017 NASW Ethics	1.05—Cultural awareness and social diversity
	1.16—Referral for services
	2.01—Respect
	2.10—Unethical conduct of colleagues
	4.01—Competence
	4.02—Discrimination
	3.01—Supervision and consultation
	5.01—Integrity of the profession
	6.04—Social and political action

Case Study	*Down but Not Out*
Primary Operating LGBTQ+ Identities	Nonbinary, femme, lesbian
Primary Operating Intersecting Identities	Immigrant, Taiwanese, student, preferred gender pronouns (they/them)
Mental/Health or Psychosocial Issues	Domestic violence, becoming/coming out/inviting in, migration, immigration/documented status, housing, depression, social support, anxiety, bilingual, family and kinship systems
Level of Practice	Micro, mezzo, macro
Nature of Practice	Generalist, MSW
2015 EPAS	2, 3, 5, 6, 7, 8
2017 NASW Ethics	1.01—Commitment to clients 1.05—Cultural awareness and social diversity 1.07—Privacy and confidentiality 1.16—Referral for services 3.01—Supervision and consultation 5.01—Integrity of the profession 6.01—Social welfare 6.04—Social and political action

Case Study	*Fostering, Forcing Choice*
Primary Operating LGBTQ+ Identities	Transgender female
Primary Operating Intersecting Identities	Teenager, African American
Mental/Health or Psychosocial Issues	Foster care, community mental health, stigma, trauma
Level of Practice	Micro, mezzo
Nature of Practice	Generalist, MSW
2015 EPAS	2, 3, 4, 6, 7, 8, 9
2017 NASW Ethics	1.01—Commitment to clients
	1.02—Self-determination
	1.05—Cultural awareness and social diversity
	1.16—Referral for services
	2.03—Interdisciplinary collaboration
	5.01—Integrity of the profession
	6.04—Social and political action

Case Study	*Love and Loss(es)*
Primary Operating LGBTQ+ Identities	Gay male, coupled
Primary Operating Intersecting Identities	Native American, married, Vietnam veteran, older/younger partner, Christian and indigenous faith
Mental/Health or Psychosocial Issues	Cancer, military service-connected disability, reservation life, health care services, family conflict, estate planning, Agent Orange

Level of Practice	Mezzo, macro
Nature of Practice	Post- / MSW
2015 EPAS	2, 3, 7, 8
2017 NASW Ethics	1.01—Commitment to clients
	1.02—Self-determination
	1.05—Cultural competence and social diversity
	1.16—Referral for services
	3.01—Supervision and consultation
	4.01—Competence
	5.01—Integrity of the profession

Case Study	*Family Dinners*
Primary Operating LGBTQ+ Identities	Nonidentified, questioning
Primary Operating Intersecting Identities	Mexican, Latino, teenager, bilingual, Catholic
Mental/Health or Psychosocial Issues	Family systems, social/media, coming out/becoming/ inviting in
Level of Practice	Micro, mezzo
Nature of Practice	Generalist
2015 EPAS	2, 3, 4, 6, 7, 8, 9
2017 NASW Ethics	1.01—Commitment to clients
	1.05—Cultural awareness and social diversity
	2.03—Interdisciplinary collaboration
	3.08—Continuing education and staff development
	5.01—Integrity of the profession

Case Study	*Never Good Enough*
Primary Operating LGBTQ+ Identities	Gay male
Primary Operating Intersecting Identities	Jewish, white, divorced, parent
Mental/Health or Psychosocial Issues	HIV+, depression, shame, abuse
Level of Practice	Micro
Nature of Practice	Post-MSW, advanced clinical
2015 EPAS	1, 2, 4, 6, 7, 8, 9
2017 NASW Ethics	1.01—Commitment to clients
	1.02—Self-determination
	1.16—Referral for services
	2.03—Interdisciplinary collaboration
	2.05—Consultation
	4.01—Competence
	5.02—Evaluation and research

Case Study	*A Good Christian Man*
Primary Operating LGBTQ+ Identities	Cisgender gay male
Primary Operating Intersecting Identities	Young adult, African American, single, Christian
Mental/Health or Psychosocial Issues	Anxiety, crisis, coming out/ becoming, minority stress, shame, intersecting oppressions
Level of Practice	Micro
Nature of Practice	Post- / MSW
2015 EPAS	2, 3, 4

2017 NASW Ethics	1.01—Commitment to clients
	1.04—Competence
	1.05—Cultural awareness and social diversity
	4.02—Discrimination
	5.01—Integrity of the profession

Case Study	*Aging Out*
Primary Operating LGBTQ+ Identities	Transgender woman, heterosexual
Primary Operating Intersecting Identities	Young person, bilingual, Puerto Rican, Ballroom Community
Mental/Health or Psychosocial Issues	Foster care, juvenile justice, congregate care, aging out, homeless, extended family, alcohol and other drugs, HIV and STI prevention
Level of Practice	Micro, mezzo, macro
Nature of Practice	Generalist, MSW
2015 EPAS	2, 3, 6, 7, 8
2017 NASW Ethics	1.01—Commitment to clients
	1.02—Self-determination
	1.05—Cultural awareness and social diversity
	3.07—Administration
	3.09—Commitments to employers
	4.01—Competence
	4.02—Discrimination
	6.01—Social welfare
	6.02—Public participation
	6.04—Social and political action

Case Study	*Suddenly Stigmatized*
Primary Operating LGBTQ+ Identities	Cisgender, lesbian
Primary Operating Intersecting Identities	Young persons, commercially sexually exploited youth, foster care
Mental/Health or Psychosocial Issues	Complex trauma, sexual exploitation, aggression, heteronormativity, minority stress, para-/suicidality
Level of Practice	Micro, mezzo, macro
Nature of Practice	Generalist, MSW
2015 EPAS	1, 2, 3, 5, 9
2017 NASW Ethics	1.01—Commitment to Clients 1.05 (a–c)—Cultural awareness and social diversity 4.01 (a–c)—Competence 2.04—Dispute involving colleague 2.09—Incompetence of colleagues 2.10—Unethical conduct of colleagues 3.01—Supervision and consultation 3.02—Education and training 3.08—Continuing education and staff development

Case Study	*Saying Goodbye:* *Re-membering Conversations*
Primary Operating LGBTQ+ Identities	Trans woman, pansexual, polyamorous
Primary Operating Intersecting Identities	White, BDSM, fetishism, kink, poly family, gay
Mental/Health or Psychosocial Issues	Neurodiverse, mood, anxiety, panic, relationship conflict
Level of Practice	Micro, mezzo
Nature of Practice	Post-/MSW, advanced clinical
2015 EPAS	2, 3, 4, 7, 8, 9
2017 NASW Ethics	1.01—Commitment to clients 1.05—Cultural awareness and social diversity 4.01—Competence 5.01—Integrity of the profession 5.02—Evaluation and research

UNIVERSAL QUESTIONS FOR ENGAGING WITH CASE STUDIES

- What other information would be helpful in your assessment and for your consideration?

  - What questions do you have?
  - What would be priority areas to explore, assess, and on which to take action?

- What are some of your existing ideas about the people in the case study as well as their identities around sexuality and gender?

- From where might these existing ideas come? How did they find their way into your life?
- In what ways are these ideas relevant or useful? How do these ideas help you to evaluate others and the world?
- How do these ideas fit into your identity as a social worker?
- In what ways might have homophobias/biphobias/transphobias, heterosexism/sexism, monosexism, cisgenderism, and heteronormativity/homonormativity/mononormativity/cisnormativity arisen for you? What about the ways in which these ideas intersect with or may be occluded or recuperated by other "-isms" and maneuvers of power, privilege, and oppression (e.g., racism, ethnocentrism, classism, white fragility, white supremacy, ableism, ageism)?
- How might you counter any essentializing, stigmatizing, or normativizing ideas?

■ Based on your standpoint and theoretical background, how might we make sense of this case?

- From an essentializing perspective, how might we make sense of this case?
- From a constructionist standpoint, how might this case be understood?

■ Considering the case on the whole, what words, ideas, behaviors, or relationship formations (among other elements) stuck out for you? How does the described lived experience(s) make sense, or not, to you?

- What images emerged when the client's identities were discussed or, quite imperatively, affirmed?

- How does this knowledge tie in with what you look for or experience in your own significant relationships? How do these ways inspire you?
- Is there a new development in how you have thought about yourself and your relationships?
- How have you been moved by being witness to this telling?

■ Which practice models or approaches might be helpful here to unpack this clinical situation as well as shed light on processing the struggles the client system is facing?

- How might you start the conversation to engage the client system?

■ Keeping intersectionality in mind, how might contemporary structural and historical factors be at play in this situation?

■ Identify and discuss your own social identities (e.g., race, sexuality, citizenship) and social locations (e.g., experiences of privilege and oppression) and how they might affect your approach to this situation and your work with this client system.

■ Which social work competencies and ethical standards provide guidance on the best way to address the issues presented? What other professional or personal ethics are important in this situation? What about other standards of care?

■ Keeping primary the principal value of social justice, how do you see your social work responsive to this case situation at the micro, mezzo, and macro levels?

- What does it look like to stand in solidarity—that is, from an allied standpoint and as an ethical guide—with this client/system?

■ How does coming to know more about some LGBTQ+ narratives fit with your assumptions?

- What new conclusions might have you reached about LGBTQ+ people and/or communities?
- From where do these ideas come? Based on whose definition of health, sexualities, genders, intimacy, risk, resilience, empowerment, justice, and beyond?
- How might these conclusions enter into how you work with LGBTQ+ people and/or communities? Equally, how might they have utility in your work with *non*-LGBTQ+ people?

REFERENCES

Adams, M., & Bell, L. A. (Eds.). (2016). *Teaching for diversity and social justice* (3rd ed.). New York, NY: Routledge.

Adams, M., Blumenfeld, W. J., Chase, D., Catalano, J., DeJong, K. S., Hackman, H. W., Hopkins, L. E., Love, B. J., Peters, M. L., Shlasko, D., & Zúñiga, X. (2018). *Readings for diversity and social justice* (4th ed.). New York, NY: Routledge.

Alessi, E. J. (2014). A framework for incorporating minority stress theory into treatment with sexual minority clients. *Journal of Gay & Lesbian Mental Health, 18*(1), 47–66.

Austin, A., Craig, S. L., Alessi, E. J., Wagaman, M. A., Paceley, M. S., Dziengel, L., & Balestrery, J. E. (2016). *Guidelines for transgender and gender nonconforming (TGNC) affirmative education: Enhancing the climate for TGNC students, staff and faculty in social work education.* Alexandria, VA: Council on Social Work Education.

Bostwick, W. B., Boyd, C. J., Hughes, T. L., & West, B. (2014). Discrimination and mental health among lesbian, gay, and bisexual adults in the United States. *American Journal of Orthopsychiatry, 84*(1), 35–45.

Brown, M. (1995). Ironies of distance: An ongoing critique of the geographies of AIDS. *Environment and Planning D: Society and Space, 13*(2), 159–183.

Council on Social Work Education (CSWE). (2015). *Educational policy and accreditation standards for baccalaureate and master's social work programs.* Alexandria, VA: Author.

Council on Social Work Education (CSWE). (2016). Position statement on conversion/reparative therapy. Retrieved from https://www.cswe.org /getattachment/Centers-Initiatives/Centers/Center-for-Diversity /About/Stakeholders/Commission-for-Diversity-and-Social-and -Economic-J/Council-on-Sexual-Orientation-and-Gender-Identity /CSOGIE-Resources/CSWEPositionStatementonConversion -ReparativeTherapy(003).pdf.aspx

Craig, S. L., Alessi, E. J., Fisher-Borne, M., Dentato, M. P., Austin, A., Paceley, M., Wagaman, A., Arguello, T., Lewis, T., Balestrery, J. E., & Van Der Horn, R. (2016). *Guidelines for affirmative social work education: Enhancing the climate for LGBQQ students, staff, and faculty in social work education.* Alexandria, VA: Council on Social Work Education.

Craig, S. L., Austin, A., & Alessi, E. (2013). Gay affirmative cognitive behavioral therapy for sexual minority youth: Clinical adaptations and approaches. *Clinical Social Work Journal, 41*(3), 258–266.

Craig, S. L., Dentato, M. P., Messinger, L., & McInroy, L. (2016). Educational determinants of readiness to practice with LGBTQ clients: Social work students speak out. *British Journal of Social Work, 46*(1), 115–134.

Craig, S. L., McInroy, L. B., Dentato, M. P., Austin, A., & Messinger, L. (2015). *Social work students speak out! The experiences of lesbian, gay, bisexual, transgender, and queer students in social work programs: A study report from the CSWE Council on Sexual Orientation and Gender Identity and Expression.* Toronto, Canada: Author.

Crisp, C., & McCave, E. L. (2007). Gay affirmative practice: A model for social work practice with gay, lesbian, and bisexual youth. *Child and Adolescent Social Work Journal, 24*(4), 403–421.

Dentato, M. (Ed.). (2017). *Social work practice with the LGBTQ community: The intersection of history, health, mental health, and politics.* New York, NY: Oxford University Press.

Dentato, M. P., Craig, S. L., Lloyd, M. R., Kelly, B. L., Wright, C., & Austin, A. (2016). Homophobia within schools of social work: The critical need for affirming classroom settings and effective preparation for service with the LGBTQ community. *Social Work Education: The International Journal, 35*(6), 672–692.

Dentato, M. P., Craig, S. L., Messinger, L., Lloyd, M., & McInroy, L. B. (2014). Outness among LGBTQ social work students in North America: The contribution of environmental supports and perceptions of comfort. *Social Work Education: The International Journal, 33*(4), 485–501.

Eells, T. D. (2015). *Psychotherapy case formulation*. Washington, DC: American Psychological Association.

Gezinski, L. (2009). Addressing sexual minority issues in social work education: A curriculum framework. *Advances in Social Work, 10*(1), 103–113.

Hicks, S., & Jeyasingham, D. (2016). Social work, queer theory and after: A genealogy of sexuality theory in neo-liberal times. *British Journal of Social Work, 46*(8), 2357–2373.

Hillcock, S., & Mulé, N. J. (Eds.). (2017). *Queering social work education*. Vancouver, Canada: UBC Press.

Hutchinson, E. D. (2014). *Dimensions of human behavior* (4th ed.). Thousand Oaks, CA: Sage.

IOM (Institute of Medicine of the National Academies). (2011). *The health of lesbian, gay, bisexual, and transgender people: Building a foundation for a better understanding*. Washington, DC: M. N. Feit, et al.

Johnson, L. M. (2014). Teaching note—heterosexism as experienced by LGBT social work educators. *Journal of Social Work Education, 50*(4), 748–751.

Love, M. M., Smith, A. E., Lyall, S. E., Mullins, J. L., & Cohn, T. J. (2015). Exploring the relationship between gay affirmative practice and empathy among mental health professionals. *Journal of Multicultural Counseling & Development, 43*(2), 83–96.

Mallon, G. P. (Ed.). (2017). *Social work practice with lesbian, gay, bisexual, and transgender people* (3rd ed.). New York, NY: Routledge.

Martin, J., Messinger, L., Kull, R., Holmes, J., Bermudez, F., & Sommer, S. (2009). *Sexual orientation and gender expression in social work education: Results from a national survey—Executive summary*. Alexandria, VA: Council on Social Work Education.

McPhail, B. (2004). Questioning gender and sexuality binaries: What queer theorists, transgendered individuals, and sex researchers can teach social work. *Journal of Gay & Lesbian Social Services, 17*(1), 3–21.

Messenger, L. (2009, September–October). Creating LGBTQ-friendly campuses. *Academe, 95*(5), 39–42.

National Association of Social Workers (NASW). (2015). *Sexual orientation change efforts (SOCE) and conversion therapy with lesbians, gay men, bisexuals and transgender persons.* Washington, DC: Author.

National Association of Social Workers (NASW). (2017). *Code of ethics of the National Association of Social Workers.* Washington, DC: Author.

National Committee on Lesbian, Gay, and Bisexual Issues. (2000). *Position statement: Reparative or conversion therapies for lesbians and gay men.* Washington, DC: Author.

Pachankis, J. E. (2014). Uncovering clinical principles and techniques to address minority stress, mental health, and related health risks among gay and bisexual men. *Clinical Psychology: Science & Practice, 21*(4), 313–330.

Papadaki, V. (2016). Invisible students: Experiences of lesbian and gay students in social work education in Greece. *Social Work Education, 35*(1), 65–77.

Polit, D. F., & Beck, C. T. (2010). Generalization in quantitative and qualitative research: Myths and strategies. *International Journal of Nursing Studies, 47*(11), 1451–1458.

Turner, G. W., Pelts, M., & Thompson, M. (2018). Between the academy and Queerness: Microaggression in social work education. *Affilia, 33*(1), 98–111.

U.S. Department of Health and Human Services. (2014). 2020 Topics & Objectives: Lesbian, gay, bisexual, and transgender health. Retrieved from https://www.healthypeople.gov/2020/topics-objectives/topic/lesbian-gay-bisexual-and-transgender-health

Wagaman, A., Shelton, J., & Carter, R. (2018). Queering the social work classroom: Strategies for increasing the inclusion of LGBTQ persons and experiences. *Journal of Teaching in Social Work, 38*(2), 166–182.

Warner, M. (2002). *Publics and counterpublics.* Brooklyn, NY: Zone Books.

1

THE "ADDICT"

George K. is a seventy-six-year-old gay, HIV+ (long-term nonprogressor), white, documented, Episcopalian, retired, cisgender man with a history of diagnosed stimulant use disorder (methamphetamines). He lives alone in an apartment in a midsize West Coast city and comfortably supports himself with a state pension and Social Security Disability Insurance income. He adheres to medical, HIV-specific, and behavioral health care and receives most of his social support from widowed, straight, cisgender women. He has no barriers to activities of daily living (ADLs) but is starting to have progressive hearing loss. He was referred to social work services at a local AIDS service organization by his new primary care provider, who, after learning about his history of meth use, has made it difficult for him to receive medical and HIV treatment unless he gets alcohol and other drug (AOD) counseling.

George grew up in the Midwest, primarily with his biological mother, who apparently suffered from severe untreated de-

---

An earlier, briefer version of this case study was presented in the pedagogical addendum of Dentato, M. (Ed.). (2017). *Social work practice with the LGBTQ community: The intersection of history, health, mental health and policy factors.* New York, NY: Oxford University Press.

pression; his biological father was absent or nonexistent during his childhood. They lived in a conservative Bible town that denounced homosexuality. George moved to California after high school. He engaged in regular sexual activity (up to multiple times per day) in various public places and gay bars during the sexual revolution and dawning of the gay rights era, from the 1960s into the early 1970s. He attended college and planned to become a high school teacher. He got caught, however, by the police in "tearoom trade" (see Humphreys, 1976), ending his teaching career before it had even started. Instead, he worked for the state in various office jobs and was a leader in regional politics.

George had an open, long-term relationship (of almost fifty years) with a man fifteen years his senior, shortly into the 2000s. His deceased partner had two daughters (now adults with their own families), who George helped parent on and off throughout their relationship. In terms of other types of relations, George reports his meth use is now infrequent and minimal in dosage, and he mostly uses it to help him perform sexually when he has the chance. He has one long-term sexual "playmate" who lives in a neighboring town and deals with his own age-related health problems. This playmate is typically the source of George's meth, as well as more recently opioid pain medication, which George reports is helpful in dealing with insomnia. George is quite expressive about the fact that he has always preferred the social and sexual company of African American men.

George has virtually no LGBTQ+ friends or social supports, except for his playmate. He is an avid reader of the *New York Times* and American and classical literature; he recently purchased a laptop and is learning about the internet. George loves the opera, although he reports he has decreased his attendance because of his progressive hearing loss. His intermittent drug use has led to tight financial times and therefore less money for the opera as well as purchasing hearing aids. He had to buy two new hearing aids within the first year of getting them, as he "misplaced them."

George has attended individual outpatient talk therapy and has engaged well in this new clinical relationship with the social worker. He has a history of attending AOD groups but recently stopped going due to his hearing loss. He has responded positively to his medical and behavioral health care. In terms of mental health, he does not meet full criteria for other major mental illnesses, and he is subclinical for mood problems. As he engages in therapy, he talks more and more about how all his friends have died of AIDS (and now more are dying because of old age), and he has never gotten to talk about living through the epidemic.

GUIDING QUESTIONS

- What other information would be helpful in your assessment and for your consideration? What questions do you have? What would be priority areas to explore and assess, and what action would you take?
- Which models or approaches might be helpful here to unpack this clinical situation as well as shed light on processing the struggles this individual is facing?
- How might you start the conversation to engage George in processing his HIV-related trauma?
- How would you approach and work with George's new primary care provider? What ethical or other obligations might you have to do so?

CASE FORMULATION

Generalist Formulation

George has lost his social support system and has engaged in problematic or possibly disordered substance use in recent years. He likely has a disordered mood due to unresolved grief, meth ab/use, and unaddressed opioid ab/use. His substance ab/use is contributing to financial difficulties and problematic engagement in care.

Culturally Responsive and Queer-Affirmative Formulation

George is a gay elder who is largely isolated on multiple levels. From a life course perspective, he belongs to a pre-Stonewall cohort of gay men who were on the front lines of the AIDS epidemic; as such, he appears to be contending with community-wide and individual trauma due to HIV/AIDS, with probable delayed onset, which has been unaddressed and therefore invalidated. While he is contending with subclinical mood symptoms, the psychosocial stressors, coupled with the unaddressed traumatic stress, may be better explained by a trauma-informed approach in assessment and differential diagnosis. In addition, his current pattern of substance mis/use appears to be an ineffective but sometimes functional method to find social connections. Compounding his current mental/physical health situation are the struggles and conflict with his primary care provider, who appears to have refrained from providing medical care and practical supports due to minimal to partial cultural knowledge of gay men generally and HIV/AIDS specifically.

TREATMENT AND ACTION PLANNING

- *Clinical case management*: George is in need of various practical supports, resources, and advocacy. These include the following:

  - Access and adherence to hearing aids
  - Home visit to more properly assess ADLs and daily living needs
  - Investigation of LGBTQ+ elderly housing options
  - Training on assistive devices to facilitate computer use (e.g., software)
  - Assessment of money management and the provision of financial literacy education
  - Cultural competency evaluation of integrated health care providers (Bidell, 2015)
  - Coordination with primary care provider and integrated health team to ensure unobstructed access to primary, gerontological, and HIV specialty care

- *AOD-related services*: George has expressed past and current problematic substance use. He shows insight and some concern.

  - Continue motivational interviewing.
  - Conduct a more thorough assessment of meth and opioid use.
  - Work with AOD group providers to assess accommodations when attending group counseling.
  - Engage with Dialectical Behavior Therapy skills to identify vulnerabilities and develop more effective coping skills for triggers (Beard et al., 2017; Dimeff & Linehan, 2008).

- Work with a primary care provider regarding sleep aids.
- Work with an integrated health team to discuss sexual health, psychoeducation, and potential sexual performance aids.

■ *Talk therapy*: George has acknowledged a number of issues that he has yet to process.

- Continue to assess mood, especially in regard to grief, while using minority stress theory (Alessi, 2014; Bostwick, Boyd, Hughes, & West, 2014; Meyer, 2003; Wight, LeBlanc, Meyer, & Harig, 2015).
- Expand assessment to include consideration of recent and historical grief related to life course cohorts regarding pre-Stonewall and HIV/AIDS histories (Cohler, 2007; Cohler & Galatzer-Levy, 2000; Hammack, 2005; McAdams, Josselson, & Lieblich, 2006).
- Engage in a narrative approach to process said histories and identity (Behan, 1999; McLean & Marini, 2008; Tilsen & Nylund, 2010).
- Engage in somatic-based mindfulness techniques as well as meaning-making strategies, based in acceptance and commitment therapy (Harris, 2006; Masuda, 2014).

■ *Committed action*: George has expressed an interest in and a need for reactivating his political past and connections with the LGBTQ+ community.

- Connect with storytelling and archiving projects, such as the GLBT Historical Society (http://www.glbthistory.org), the HIV Story Project (www.thehivstoryproject.org), or Let's Kick ASS (www.letskickass.hiv).

- Connect with LGBTQ+ elder/older advocacy groups, networking, housing support, and other resources via SAGE (www.sageusa.org).

- Connect with a speakers bureau regarding HIV+ or LGBTQ+ people, possibly operating through local universities and AIDS service organizations.

- Connect with peer-to-peer emotional support; for example, see the Shanti Project (www.shanti.org).

REFERENCES AND RESOURCES

Alessi, E. J. (2014). A framework for incorporating minority stress theory into treatment with sexual minority clients. *Journal of Gay & Lesbian Mental Health, 18,* 47–66.

Beard, C., Kirakosian, N., Silverman, A. L., Winer, J. P., Wadsworth, L. P., & Björgvinsson, T. (2017). Comparing treatment response between LGBQ and heterosexual individuals attending a CBT- and DBT-skills-based partial hospital. *Journal of Consulting and Clinical Psychology, 85*(12), 1171–1181.

Behan, C. (1999). Linking lives around shared themes: Narrative group therapy with gay men. *Gecko, 2,* 18–34.

Bidell, M. (2015). Using the Sexual Orientation Counselor Competency Scale (SOCCS) in mental health and healthcare settings: An instructor's guide. *MedEdPORTAL Publications, 11,* 10040.

Bostwick, W. B., Boyd, C. J., Hughes, T. L., & West, B. (2014). Discrimination and mental health among lesbian, gay, and bisexual adults in the United States. *American Journal of Orthopsychiatry, 84*(1), 35–45.

Cohler, B. J. (2007). *Writing desire: Sixty years of gay autobiography.* Madison: University of Wisconsin Press.

Cohler, B. J., & Galatzer-Levy, R. M. (2000). *The course of gay and lesbian lives: Social and psychoanalytic perspectives.* Chicago, IL: University of Chicago Press.

Dimeff, L. A., & Linehan, M. M. (2008). Dialectical behavior therapy for substance abusers. *Addiction Science & Clinical Practice, 4*(2), 39–47.

Hammack, P. L. (2005). The life course development of human sexual orientation: An integrative paradigm. *Human Development, 48,* 267–290.

Harris, R. (2006). Embracing your demons: An overview of acceptance and commitment therapy. *Psychotherapy in Australia, 12*(4), 2–8.

Humphreys, L. (1976). *Tearoom trade: Impersonal sex in public places.* New York, NY: Routledge.

Masuda, A. (2014). *Mindfulness & acceptance in multicultural competency: A contextual approach to sociocultural diversity in theory & practice.* Oakland, CA: New Harbinger.

McAdams, D. P., Josselson, R., & Lieblich, A. (Eds.). (2006). *Identity and story: Creating self in narrative.* Washington, DC: American Psychological Association.

McLean, R., & Marini, I. (2008). Working with gay men from a narrative counseling perspective: A case study. *Journal of LGBT Issues in Counseling, 2*(3), 243–257.

Meyer, I. H. (2003). Prejudice, social stress, and mental health in lesbian, gay, and bisexual populations: Conceptual issues and research evidence. *Psychological Bulletin, 129*(5), 674–697.

Tilsen, J., & Nylund, D. (2010). Resisting normativity: Queer musings on politics, identity, and the performance of therapy. *International Journal of Narrative Therapy and Community Work, 3,* 64–70.

Wight, R. G., LeBlanc, A. J., Meyer, I. H., & Harig, F. A. (2015). Internalized ageism, mattering, and depressive symptoms among midlife and older gay-identified men. *Social Science & Medicine, 147,* 200–208.

2

EMPLOYEE ASSISTANCE PROGRAM

TAMECA N. HARRIS-JACKSON

April is a forty-year-old African American cisgender woman seeking counseling services through her company's employee assistance program (EAP) due to job dissatisfaction. April is referred to Lynn, an EAP social worker, and they agree to meet for a sixty-minute intake session.

During the intake, April reveals that she is an attorney at a prestigious law firm in Chicago. She is the middle child of three siblings. Her older brother is a physician who spends much of his time working overseas, and her younger sister is an accomplished violinist. When discussing her family background, Lynn notices that April's face lights up. April shares that she comes from a "proud" family and that she and her siblings were raised in Alabama. Her mother worked part-time as a nurse, and her father worked long hours as a manager of a mail distribution center. April states that her parents "took education seriously" and that she and her siblings graduated at the top of their high school class. April and her siblings went on to attend prestigious universities across the country.

Despite achieving such high honors, April expresses that she does not feel that she receives the recognition that she deserves from supervisors and colleagues. She states that to deal with this feeling, she often works even harder to "prove" that she is capable and does belong at the firm. She states that the success of her and her siblings is a way to honor their parents for all of the sacrifices that they have made for them. April states that when she was offered a position with her current firm, she felt that she was "on top of the world" and that she "had finally arrived."

April reports that she has been with the firm for six years, and she acknowledges that she has had many successes. She states that she has an excellent track record of winning cases and a solid reputation among her peers. She reports that there are six partners at the firm and seven junior associates. Four of the partners are white men and two are white women. All of the seven associates are white except for April and another woman, who is of Southeast Asian descent. April states she hates the fact that she has to even consider these variables when discussing her job stress, but "nothing else makes sense" to her. Specifically, when there are discussions about promotions to partner, April states that she is not even considered. She states she has inquired about this a few times, but each time she feels she is "passively dismissed" or "made to feel paranoid" for asking. April goes on to say that while she can prove nothing, it just feels as if her colleagues are purposely overlooking her. For instance, during a most recent discussion, the two senior attorneys shared names for consideration for promotion to partner. April was not included as a candidate, and furthermore, those names included people with less time with the firm and fewer wins than April. April states she discussed this with one of the senior partners, who stated, "Well, I didn't think you were interested in staying on. I gathered you might want to venture off on your own at some point. Maybe do some work in your community?" April looks at Lynn and screams, "I can't for the life of me imagine why he would think this! I've been there for six years, and I have never said I wanted to leave. I've even started a pro bono project to bring more awareness to the firm for Christ's sake!"

April states that for the past year, she has been sharing her frustrations with her siblings as well as her husband and wife, but she feels that everyone is tired of hearing her complain. Recently, her brother and sister have been "too busy" to take her calls, and both her husband and wife told her to "just get over it or leave the firm already." April shares with Lynn that over the past several weeks, she has found it "more and more difficult to get out of bed." She has called in sick to work several times, which is "completely unlike" her. She proceeds to tell Lynn that she just lies in bed most days, has trouble eating and sleeping, and cannot pull herself out of it. She also feels that she just wants to "shut down" because she feels no one seems to understand her. She shares that she feels tired of fighting and trying to prove herself.

After writing some notes, Lynn looks at a tearful April and says, "I just want to go back a minute. You said your husband *and* wife, is that right?" April responds yes, adding that they have been married for eight years. Lynn pauses and states that she is confused. She then asks how April can be married to both a man and a woman. April goes on to explain that she is in a polyamorous relationship, meaning that her family includes more than one committed spouse in the relationship. April goes on to say that she does not feel very supported by them right now. Lynn then moves closer to April and asks, "Well, are you bisexual then? I don't understand." April states that at one point in her life, she did identify as bisexual, but now she just identifies as someone who loves her two spouses. April attempts to share more about her job issues, but Lynn continues to ask questions about the relationship: "How does the relationship work? Do you all sleep in the same bed? Does anyone get jealous?" April exhales, sits back in her chair, and matter-of-factly answers Lynn's questions. In the middle of one of April's responses, Lynn looks down at her watch and says, "My goodness! We are over time. We need to stop here. But I'd like to arrange another meeting for us, so we can talk more about your relationship and the other things that are bothering you." However, April quickly responds by telling Lynn that she doesn't think another appointment will be necessary.

GUIDING QUESTIONS

- In what ways may it be important to conceptualize April's issues through an intersectional lens? Describe.
- Does April's situation require Lynn to be able to bridge practice and policy? If yes, how can Lynn go about doing this?
- How do you respond to April's concerns about being overlooked for a promotion because she is a person of color?
- What do you think about Lynn's decision to focus on April's relationship? Based on Lynn's questions, do you think she did an effective job of managing her countertransference? If yes, explain why? If not, what do you think Lynn could have done better?
- If it has not occurred in your practice experience yet, how can you imagine maintaining a safe, therapeutic space for clients who disclose behaviors, sexual and otherwise, that are difficult for you yourself—due to your own social location, politics, identities, or other partial knowledge? If these experiences have arisen for you, how have you maintained your professionalism and conducted competent practice in best service of your client?

■ How would you respond to a colleague, who you may be consulting with individually or in group supervision, behaving in such a manner?

CASE FORMULATION

Generalist Formulation

April is dealing with work-related problems that have negatively affected her mood. Specifically, she believes that she has been overlooked for a promotion because she is a racial minority. She reports symptoms consistent with major depressive disorder, including depressed mood for more than two weeks, trouble eating and sleeping, and difficulty engaging in pleasurable activities. In addition, she reports interpersonal distress. She feels her husband, wife, and siblings are tired of hearing her complain about her work-related problems. They suggest she either quit her job or just stay and stop discussing it.

Culturally Responsive and Queer-Affirmative Formulation

April is an African American woman struggling with depressive symptoms related to her job. She feels her supervisors do not recognize her success and in turn believes this is because she is a woman of color. She has noted experiencing microaggressions and the symptoms that generally follow (e.g., feelings of uncertainty related to identifying as feeling marginalized and/ or discriminated against based on aspects of identity). Her employers have not taken her concerns seriously and refuse to examine how structural forces may inadvertently contribute to the marginalization of people of color in the workplace. Her employers may assume that hiring people of color, such as April, automatically suggests that they do not discriminate against diverse groups. However, organizations must strive for not only diversity but also inclusion.

Furthermore, April's social worker, Lynn, has difficulty engaging in culturally competent practice with April. When she discovers that April is in a polyamorous relationship, Lynn switches the focus of the session to April's relationship. She starts to ask April numerous questions that appear to be rather irrelevant since April is not presenting for treatment regarding relationship conflict per se. Also, Lynn tries to educate herself about polyamorous relationships by bombarding April with numerous questions. To be a LGBTQ+ affirmative practitioner, social workers should not rely on their clients to answer all of their questions about specific relationships that do not conform to monogamy or heterosexuality. Every relationship and identity are unique to the individual, and clients are the best source to define what their identities and relationships mean to them. Parallel to the clinical work conducted with the client (system), social workers must be committed to doing their own work to educate themselves about the various forms of human relationships and sexual identities that exist beyond heteronormativity and monogamy.

TREATMENT AND ACTION PLANNING

Although the client in this case is presenting with sincere concern related to a probable depressive disorder, a more significant aspect of treatment for this case rests in the clinician's ability and willingness to engage in introspection, self-regulation, continuing education, and supervision to effectively assist this client or future clients who present with similar identities. As a result, treatment and action planning will focus on the needs of the clinician. This includes the following:

- *Self-awareness and professionalism*: The clinician in this case is having difficulty demonstrating a commitment to the client due to an inability to engage in self-regulation. Specifically, the clinician's failure to manage her affective reactions related to the client's sexual orientation and relationship status results in a demonstration of poor professional demeanor as evidenced by negating the client's presenting issues of a stressful work environment and depressive mood. Instead, the clinician proceeds to bombard the client with questions about the nature, style, and content of her relationship, demonstrating a lack of knowledge with regard to LGBTQ+ identities and the multitude of human relationship styles that exist. Therefore, a part of the treatment plan for this case would require the clinician to engage in self-awareness/reflection and explore issues of countertransference and self-regulation. Specifically, the clinician would want to be able to recognize how the problematic behaviors (e.g., too much interest in nonpresenting case issues of the client's life) could impede the therapeutic relationship with the client (Schaverien, 2006). In addition, the clinician may wish to engage in supervision and consultation to aid in processing her own feelings related to LGBTQ+ identities and nonmonogamy, as well as engage in continuing education related to these topics to enhance her knowledge and competence in this area.
- *Racial, ethnic, and cultural competence*: The clinician in this case is having difficulty being present with the client. She also failed to affirm the client's concerns. Specifically, the clinician failed

to express understanding of the client's cultural background as an African American woman growing up in a region of the United States noted for deep racial/cultural division, oppression, and discrimination toward black Americans. The ability of the clinician to recognize and affirm the client's lifelong experiences and feeling of having to "prove" herself and her worth as a black American is key and critical to developing an effective therapeutic relationship. Therefore, an additional part of the treatment plan would require the clinician to (1) seek a deeper understanding of the client's cultural background to work toward providing support, and (2) communicate understanding regarding the importance of diversity and difference in shaping life experiences. Such practices by the clinician would highlight the theoretical framework of critical race theory (CRT), which embraces and challenges awareness, understanding, and the role of race as part of how we engage one another in society, whether through hidden biases or overt practices. CRT also acknowledges how power and privilege affect individual and collective experiences, as well as how historically marginalized and oppressed identities are not limited to just race but include, for this case, gender and orientation and the difficulty navigating those multiple or intersectional identities in society (Delgado & Stefancic, 2001).

■ *Effective engagement*: In this case, the clinician failed to use empathy, reflection, and interpersonal skills to effectively engage the client. As noted toward the end of the session, the clinician's inability to engage in self-regulation resulted in the need to abruptly end the session without providing affirmation of the client's presenting issues or expressing empathy regarding the client's concerns. Furthermore, as a matter of assessment, the clinician should apply knowledge of theoretical frameworks to aid with client engagement, such as black feminist theory (Collins, 2009), and subsequently collect and organize data to interpret information (e.g., sociocultural factors resulting in a manifestation of depressive symptoms). Following successful engagement, the clinician should endeavor to collaborate with the client to develop mutually agreed-upon goals that may abate depressive symptoms (e.g., continuing talk therapy to aid with processing, role-playing self-advocacy with agency partners, and weighing pro/cons of alternate work environments and what leaving the job to pursue alternate options may mean to the client).

■ *Interpersonal effectiveness:* Finally, as a method of action, self-awareness and an apology to the client are needed from the clinician. If the clinician presents an inability to effectively engage in the above self-treatment and action items, an advised action would be for the clinician to engage in a warm handoff (i.e., referral) of the client to someone who is best able to meet the client's therapeutic needs. Subsequently, the clinician should aim to follow the treatment plan above related to introspection, continuing education, and supervision to be of best aid in future cases.

REFERENCES AND RESOURCES

Abrams, L. S., & Moio, J. A. (2009). Critical race theory and the cultural competence dilemma in social work education. *Journal of Social Work Education, 45,* 245–261.

Alessi, E. J. (2014). A framework for incorporating minority stress theory into treatment with sexual minority clients. *Journal of Gay & Lesbian Mental Health, 18,* 47–66.

Collins, P. H. (2009). *Black feminist thought.* New York, NY: Routledge.

Conley, T. D., Moors, A. C., Matsick, J. L., & Ziegler, A. (2013). The fewer the merrier? Assessing stigma surrounding consensually non-monogamous romantic relationships. *Analyses of Social Issues and Public Policy, 13,* 1–30.

Delgado, R., & Stefancic, J. (2001). *Critical race theory: An introduction*. New York, NY: New York University Press.

Jordan-Zachery, J. (2007). Am I a black woman or a woman who is black? A few thoughts on the meaning of intersectionality. *Politics and Gender, 3*(2), 254–263.

Morrison, T. G., Beaulieu, D., Brockman, M., & Beaglaoich, C. Ó. (2013). A comparison of polyamorous and monoamorous persons: Are there differences in indices of relationship well-being and sociosexuality? *Psychology & Sexuality, 1*, 75–91.

National Association of Social Workers. (2001). Standards and indicators for cultural competence in social work practice. Retrieved from http://www.socialworkers.org/practice/standards/NASWculturalstandards.pdf

Satterly, B., & Ingersoll, T. (2016). *Sexuality concepts for social workers*. San Diego, CA: Cognella.

Schaverien, J. (2006). *Gender, countertransference and the erotic transference: Perspectives from analytical psychology and psychoanalysis*. New York, NY: Routledge.

Sue, D. W., & Sue, D. (2016). *Counseling the culturally diverse: Theory and practice* (7th ed.). Hoboken, NJ: Wiley.

Weitzman, G. (2010). Therapy with clients who are bisexual and polyamorous. *Journal of Bisexuality, 6*, 137–164.

Wosick-Correa, C. (2010). Agreements, rules and agentic fidelity in polyamorous relationships. *Psychology & Sexuality, 1*, 41–61.

3

TRANS-ITIONING, AGAIN

TYLER M. ARGÜELLO

Donald is a forty-six-year-old, African American, trans masculine gay male. He is an allied clinical provider with a graduate degree, and he has been a political advocate and leader in LGBTQ+ rights alongside having worked in AIDS service organizations. He moved from a major city two years ago, has a strong social network mostly outside this current midsized town in the Northwest, owns a new home, has a dog, and works out regularly.

Donald presents for outpatient therapy after being diagnosed with HIV one month prior and knowing he was infected four months before that. He is engaged in and adherent to medical care and an HIV clinical trial; currently, his HIV is undetectable, with an increasing T-cell count, and no related problems to HIV. He has a history of type 1 diabetes mellitus and wears an insulin pump; this is largely under control, although day to day he has more regular problems with his diabetes (versus HIV). He maintains routine gynecological care, has no history of pregnancies, and is entering menopause. He transitioned in his mid-twenties, after living as a "butch lesbian" during teen and college years (at a women's college). During that time, he experienced major depression, engaged in some self-harming behaviors, and contemplated suicide, which resulted in an extended inpatient psychiatric stay. Since his mid-twenties, he has lived openly as a gay man, has a history of hormone therapy, completed one top surgery, has had a few long-term relationships, and has become a health care professional.

Currently, he is considering a (second) top revision surgery and has expressed interest in possible bottom surgery, as there have been some surgical advances since his first procedure over twenty years ago. He has been in psychotherapy on and off throughout his life, previously has taken antidepressant medication (but not currently), and uses sleeping pills as needed. He has some communication with his family, who all live in the rural South. His biological father died many years ago; his biological mother lives alone and has a history of alcohol abuse and emotionally abusive tendencies. He has a sister and a brother who have partners and children of their own. The family is generally supportive of his identities, yet they are not particularly encouraging or public in their own communities about these topics. In terms of family, Donald has embraced the idea of parenting but is too shy to openly admit such goals; still, he is beginning to investigate options for fostering or adopting LGBTQ+ teenagers from the region who are in the child welfare system.

Donald reports that he has a long history of engaging with gay social media for finding sexual partners; as of late, he is using them more for socializing. Typically, he will have weekly or biweekly sexual encounters, which are sometimes anonymous; he prefers partners with whom he has some experience. He has some regular partners who are cis-gay as well as cis-hetero men, some in open relationships and some in heterosexual marriages. Donald reports that he has a long history of engaging in unprotected vaginal intercourse and sometimes anal intercourse. Prior to and since his HIV diagnosis, it was not a routine practice for

Donald to discuss his partner's or his status of sexually transmitted infections. Donald's chief concern in engaging with therapy this time is, "How could this happen to me?"

GUIDING QUESTIONS

- What other information would be helpful in your assessment and for your consideration? What questions do you have?
- Without burdening the client, how would you educate yourself and increase your cultural responsiveness about matters of trans health and mental health care in this case?
- What ways would be most effective to build quick rapport and provide traction to establish a strong therapeutic alliance?
- What would be priority areas to explore, assess, and on which to take action? What would be short-term as well as long-term goals and objectives in this case?
- As the social worker is seeing Donald in a private practice environment, which strategies should be used to engage with various other providers and ultimately create and maintain an integrated care team and culture among disparate providers?

CASE FORMULATION

Generalist Formulation

Donald is a middle-aged, black, gay, trans man with chronic medical and psychosocial problems. He has difficulty with personal attachments and has exhibited codependent traits in his intimate relationships—an ultimate expression of which could be having unprotected intercourse with his partners. More often, he has relied on impersonal methods for closeness with other gay men, which reinforces his feeling apart from "the (gay) community" and a "true" (gay) man. And, now, with his recent HIV infection, this new situation compounds the longstanding shame around always having felt like a "problem" and cognitively fusing with the thought that he is a "not well" person.

Culturally Responsive and Queer-Affirmative Formulation

Donald is a man who, for the majority of his formative development and more generally across his life, has lived within heavily stigmatized environments and communities replete with multiple layers of invalidation. Earlier on, he endured being overparentalized by his abusive mother, who reportedly struggled with severe emotional dysregulation and alcohol abuse. From when he was a young teenager through young adulthood, he found himself coping to the best of his abilities (largely on his own) with intersecting racism, homophobia, misogyny, and transphobia. Staying well has been chronically difficult because he was left to largely fend for himself with his diabetes, the sum of which often eclipsed his psychosocial struggles in coming into his sexuality and gender identity and expression. As he has become empowered with those identities, he has had to contend with the sexual racism (see, e.g., Han, 2007) amid the gay community, so as he has attempted to increase his sexual pleasure and connectedness with gay men, he receives some reinforcement and continued objectification for being black and trans. And while he has engaged with a variety of well-founded prevention strategies, this recent change in his serostatus has pushed him into despair and self-persecution. Accordingly, given his multiply marginalized social position, there inheres an "inevitability" for him to become HIV positive.

TREATMENT AND ACTION PLANNING

- *Clinician praxis, reflexivity*: Donald continues to contend with potential conflicts and struggles with receiving effective access and competent care. Similarly, clinicians (and any future specialists or care providers) are faced with providing competent care and contending with various issues of countertransference. Therefore, clinicians can take several steps to support Donald as well as empower themselves:

  - During any processing around body modifications and other trans health care issues, the clinician should be mindful to avoid objectifying the client and inappropriately focusing on his body and body parts. To that end, engaging with relevant continuing education courses and consultation is necessary, especially regarding trans health care, knowledge, and awareness:
    - o Visit the World Professional Association for Transgender Health and examine the *Standards of Care* at www.wpath .org.
    - o Consult practicing expert clinicians, for example, https:// darlenetandogenderblog.com.
  - Engage with a critical and intersectional standpoint to attend to Donald's multiple identities, appreciating the differences and conflicts that LGBTQ+ people of color face. From there, gain an understanding of how continual identity negotiation may affect stress, health, and well-being (Crawford,

Allison, Zamboni, & Soto, 2002; Hammoud-Becket, 2007; Walters, Evans-Campbell, Simoni, Ronquillo, & Bhuyan, 2006; Walters & Simoni, 1993).

■ *Trans emergence model*: Related to the point above, it would be necessary to explore how HIV treatment squares with trans health care and continued identity formation. The clinician can function as an advocate in the multidisciplinary treatment team to increase cultural competence and work against stigma, especially in the tendencies fostered by psychiatric diagnoses.

Lev (2004) provides the transgender emergence model, a staged model that looks at how trans people come to understand their identity, crafted from a clinical point of view asserting processes for both the individual and responsibilities for the clinician: awareness, seeking information/reaching out, disclosure to significant others, exploration of identity and self-labeling, exploration of transition and body modification, and integration or acceptance and posttransition issues.

■ *Ecological model*: In processing Donald's thoughts and feelings about HIV and his sexuality as a gay man, it may be helpful to engage with the ecological model, which builds off of social identity theory (see Alderson, 2003; Cox & Gallois, 1996) by grounding development in an ecological paradigm: human development derives from individuals themselves, their environments, and the reciprocal interactions between the two. The focus here is on identity acquisition, which is one way to further manifest a gay-affirmative standpoint. LGBTQ+ identities are a critical example of identification in practice, that is, making sense of some attribute portrayed as immutable yet reflexively realized over the life span and various spaces (Rowe, 2014).

Progressively, the degree to which one can experience and live out their identity is correlated with well-being and health promotion (see Hudson, 2015).

- *Life course approach*: In addition to the ecological model, it may be effective to engage with an approach that reconciles Donald's struggles with having a long-standing history of being in an "AIDS cohort," surviving long term, and now being infected (Cohler, 2007; Cohler & Galatzer-Levy, 2000; Elder, 1998; Hammack, 2005; Kimmel, 1990; McAdams, Josselson, & Lieblich, 2006).

- *Technology and communication*: Countering stigmatizing perspectives around social media and avenues for networking, a functional perspective may be helpful in processing advantages of online activities and bridging them to effective real-time encounters and relationships. For LGBTQ+ people in general, especially the emerging generation saturated with multimedia, online communities can be critical safe(r) spaces to provide knowledge, connections, and increased self-acceptance (Browne, Lim, & Brown, 2009; Downing, 2013; Gross, 2004; Harper, Bruce, Serrano, & Jamil, 2009; Huffaker & Calvert, 2005; Kraut et al., 1998; McKenna & Bargh, 1998; Mesch & Talmud, 2006; Schmitt, Dayanim, & Matthias, 2008; Turow, 1999; Valkenburg & Peter, 2008).

  - Pragmatically, clinical interventions that have functional or contextual analysis and that promote behavior change can be effective in practice. For example, acceptance and commitment therapy can foster attention to values-based processing and linking that to committed action during sexual and social encounters (Plumb, Stewart, Dahl, & Lundgren, 2009; Skinta, 2014; Skinta & Curtin, 2016).

- Similarly, dialectical behavior therapy facilitates pragmatic engagement with helpful coping skills and effective behavioral strategies related to interpersonal effectiveness, which may facilitate communicating with (sexual) partners, engaging in a satisfying primary relationship, and coaching around the foster/adoption process (Boone, 2014; Masuda, 2014; Rizvi, Steffel, & Carson-Wong, 2012).

■ *Positive/affirmative HIV-positive care*: As it is imperative to provide a gay-affirmative environment, it is necessary to tend to the affirmation of Donald's serostatus. This may be facilitated in clinical treatment through the methods and perspectives delineated above. As well, it would be important to facilitate and advocate for connections into local, regional, and national communities, albeit in ways that are aligned with Donald's values and interests. Some resources could be AIDS life cycle (biking) or walk/run events, support groups at LGBT centers or HIV/AIDS service organizations, or peer support networks (e.g., www.shanti.org). Given that Donald's social networks are afar, increasing support (via social media and video chats) could be useful.

  It is important to note that, when working with transmasculine men, there is still a dearth of literature specifically for those who may identify as gay, bisexual, or men who have sex with men. Recent limited data show similar risk factors to their cisgender counterparts, including histories of childhood sexual abuse, depression, and stimulant use (Scheim, Bauer, & Travers, 2017).

■ *Clinical case management*: It may be important to engage with Donald's care team, that is, HIV care, medical (diabetes) care, gynecological care, and trans health care. In addition, social work is aptly suited to conduct ongoing psychoeducation regarding safer sex practices and risk reduction (see, e.g., Holosko, 2018).

- Gay and Lesbian Medical Association, http://www.glma.org
- Centers for Disease Control and Prevention: HIV among Gay and Bisexual Men, http://www.cdc.gov/hiv/group/msm
- Centers for Disease Control and Prevention: Gay and Bisexual Men's Resources, http://www.cdc.gov/msmhealth/professional-resources.htm

REFERENCES AND RESOURCES

Alderson, K. G. (2003). The ecological model of gay male identity. *Canadian Journal of Human Sexuality, 12*(2), 75–85.

Boone, M. S. (Ed.). (2014). *Mindfulness & acceptance in social work*. Oakland, CA: New Harbinger.

Browne, K., Lim, J., & Brown, G. (Eds.). (2009). *Geographies of sexualities: Theory, practices and politics*. Surrey, UK: Ashgate.

Cohler, B. J. (2007). *Writing desire: Sixty years of gay autobiography*. Madison: University of Wisconsin Press.

Cohler, B. J., & Galatzer-Levy, R. M. (2000). *The course of gay and lesbian lives: Social and psychoanalytic perspectives*. Chicago, IL: University of Chicago Press.

Cox, S., & Gallois, C. (1996). Gay and lesbian identity development: A social identity perspective. *Journal of Homosexuality, 30*(4), 1–30.

Crawford, I., Allison, K. W., Zamboni, B. D., & Soto. T. (2002). The influence of dual-identity development on the psychosocial functioning of African-American gay and bisexual men. *Journal of Sex Research, 39,* 179–189.

Downing, G. (2013). Virtual youth: Non-heterosexual young people's use of the Internet to negotiate their identities and socio-sexual relations. *Children's Geographies, 11*(1), 44–58.

Elder, G. H., Jr. (1998). The life course as developmental theory. *Child Development, 69,* 1–12.

Gross, E. F. (2004). Adolescent Internet use: What we expect, what teens report. *Journal of Applied Developmental Psychology, 25*(6), 633–649.

Hammack, P. L. (2005). The life course development of human sexual orientation: An integrative paradigm. *Human Development, 48,* 267–290.

Hammoud-Becket, S. (2007). *Azima ila hayati*—an invitation in to my life: Narrative conversations about sexual identity. *International Journal of Narrative Therapy and Community Work, 1,* 29–39.

Han, C.-S. (2007). They don't want to cruise your type: Gay men of color and the racial politics of exclusion. *Social Identities, 13*(1), 51–67.

Harper, G. W., Bruce, D., Serrano, P., & Jamil, O. B. (2009). The role of the Internet in the sexual identity development of gay and bisexual male adolescents. In P. L. Hammack & B. J. Cohler (Eds.), *The story of sexual identity: Narrative perspectives on the gay and lesbian life course* (pp. 297–326). Oxford, UK: Oxford University Press.

Holosko, M. J. (2018). *Social work case management: Case studies from the frontlines.* Thousand Oaks, CA: Sage.

Hudson, K. D. (2015). Toward a conceptual framework for understanding community belonging and well-being: Insights from a queer-mixed perspective. *Journal of Community Practice, 23*(1), 27–50.

Huffaker, D. A., & Calvert, S. L. (2005). Gender, identity, and language use in teenage blogs. *Journal of Computer-Mediated Communication, 10*(2). Retrieved from https://onlinelibrary.wiley.com/toc/10836101/2005/10/2

Kimmel, D. C. (1990). *Adulthood and aging* (3rd ed.). New York, NY: Wiley.

Kraut, R., Patterson, M., Lundmark, V., Kiesler, S., Mukophadhyay, T., & Scherlis, W. (1998). Internet paradox: A social technology that reduces social involvement and psychological well-being? *American Psychologist, 53,* 1017–1031.

Lev, A. I. (2004). *Transgender emergence: Therapeutic guidelines for working with gender-variant people and their families.* New York, NY: Haworth.

Masuda, A. (Ed.). (2014). *Mindfulness & acceptance in multicultural competence: A contextual approach to sociocultural diversity in theory & practice.* Oakland, CA: New Harbinger.

McAdams, D. P., Josselson, R., & Lieblich, A. (Eds.). (2006). *Identity and story: Creating self in narrative.* Washington, DC: American Psychological Association.

McKenna, K. Y. A., & Bargh, J. A. (1998). Coming out in the age of the Internet: Identity "demarginalization" through virtual group participation. *Journal of Personality and Social Psychology, 75*(3), 681–694.

Mesch, G., & Talmud, I. (2006). The quality of online and offline relationships: The role of multiplexity and duration of social relationships. *The Information Society, 22,* 137–148.

Plumb, J. C., Stewart, I., Dahl, J., & Lundgren, T. (2009). In search of meaning: Values in modern clinical behavior analysis. *The Behavior Analyst, 32,* 85–103.

Rizvi, S. L., Steffel, L. M., & Carson-Wong, A. (2012). Overview of dialectical behavior therapy for professional psychologists. *Professional Psychology: Research and Practice, 44*(92), 73–80.

Rowe, M. (2014). Becoming and belonging in gay men's life stories: A case study of a voluntaristic model of identity. *Sociological Perspectives, 57*(4), 434–449.

Scheim, A. I., Bauer, G. R., & Travers, R. (2017). HIV-related sexual risk among transgender men who are gay, bisexual, or have sex with men. *Journal of Acquired Immune Deficiency Syndrome, 74*(4), e89–e96.

Schmitt, K. L., Dayanim, S., & Matthias, S. (2008). Personal homepage construction as an expression of social development. *Developmental Psychology, 44*(2), 496–506.

Skinta, M. D. (2014). Acceptance- and compassion-based approaches for invisible minorities: Working with shame among sexual minorities. In A. Masuda (Ed.), *Mindfulness & acceptance in multicultural competence: A contextual approach to sociocultural diversity in theory & practice* (pp. 213–225). Oakland, CA: New Harbinger.

Skinta, M. D., & Curtin, A. (Eds.). (2016). *Mindfulness & acceptance for gender & sexual minorities: A clinician's guide to fostering compassion, connection & equality using contextual strategies.* Oakland, CA: New Harbinger.

Turow, J. (1999). *The Internet and the family: The view from the parents—the view from the press* (Report Series No. 27). Philadelphia: Annenberg Public Policy Center of the University of Pennsylvania.

Valkenburg, P. M., & Peter, J. (2008). Adolescents' identity experiments on the Internet: Consequences for social competence and self-concept unity. *Communication Research, 35*(2), 208–231.

Walters, K. L., Evans-Campbell, T., Simoni, J., Ronquillo, T., & Bhuyan, R. (2006). "My spirit in my heart": Identity experiences and challenges among American Indian Two-Spirit women. *Journal of Lesbian Studies, 10*(1/2), 125–149.

Walters, K. L., & Simoni, J. M. (1993). Lesbian and gay male group identity attitudes and self-esteem: Implications for counseling. *Journal of Counseling Psychology, 40,* 94–99.

4

TRYING TO CONCEIVE

JUDITH LEITCH

Shira is a thirty-five-year-old white, able-bodied cisgender woman who identifies as a lesbian. Shira presents in therapy stating that she does not have major problems in her life, characterizing her life as "generally good." However, she states that she "wants to be prepared" and has the ambiguous goal of "having someone to talk to beyond burdening friends." To that point, Shira relays that her core motivation to engage in individual therapy has arisen from her struggle with fertility over the past eighteen months.

Shira has been married to Aviva, who is thirty years old, for five years. Both women live and work in Washington, DC. They are high-earning professionals, with high-pressure jobs that typically require fifty or more hours of work per week. This marriage is Aviva's first. Alternatively, Shira was previously married when she was twenty-eight for less than one year. Shira's ex-wife was substantially older than her, and the couple split up because of her ex's reluctance to start a family.

Shira comes from a small, middle-class family consisting of her parents, a schoolteacher (her mother) and a nurse (her father). Her sister, Rachel, who is two years older, is a lobbyist with a prestigious firm located near Shira's job with the federal government. Shira grew up in a small, wealthy suburb of Washington, in which she was able to develop close relationships with peers at her Jewish private school, which Rachel also attended. After Rachel left for college, Shira became involved in volunteer efforts to rebuild New Orleans after Hurricane Katrina. After that, she attended college at a small midwestern liberal arts school, where she studied public policy and advocacy. After graduation, she moved back to Washington to attend a Master of Public Policy program, and has lived there since.

Shira reports that she is close with her family of origin, chatting with her mother by phone three or four times per week and participating in a family group text message chain. Shira spends time with her or Aviva's family on major holidays, as well as shares an annual "sisters only" vacation with Rachel. Shira admires Rachel and Rachel's husband, Milton, and sometimes compares her life with Aviva unfavorably to Rachel and Milton because they have more financial resources and social prestige. Shira says that Aviva talks with her own family about more superficial and cerebral topics and that Aviva's family is more rationally focused while Shira sees her own family as "warmer." Shira consults with her family before any major decisions, often asking her mother's opinion before she seeks out Aviva's.

Shira has been out as a lesbian to her family since the middle of high school and states that her family is "supportive" of her sexuality but also "uninterested" in its importance to her. Shira's parents currently do not have any grandchildren, and while they both claim they will "be excited whenever it happens," Shira feels strongly that they would like both her and Rachel to have children as soon as possible. Both Shira and Aviva identify as Jewish and come from Ashkenazi Jewish heritage. Shira describes herself as "culturally Jewish but not religious," celebrating Jewish holidays, traditions, and community but finding little meaning in the spiritual practices of Judaism. Shira is aware that Jewish traditions mandate "being fruitful and multiplying." Although Shira reports she does not feel affected by this, she does feel that being raised in a culture that emphasizes family building has likely shaped her values and goals.

Shira and Aviva have been trying to conceive for the past eighteen months. Shira is determined to carry the pregnancy, although she has been diagnosed with polycystic ovary syndrome and is a carrier for Tay-Sachs disease. Shira expresses specific interest in being the gestational mother due to a long-standing desire to be pregnant as well as to have a prenatal connection to her child. Shira and Aviva have talked about different ways to build a family, and they have agreed they want Shira to be inseminated with an anonymous, Jewish sperm donor. The two have agreed on a donor, fertility clinic, and doctor for this process. At this time, Shira has been inseminated through intrauterine insemination (IUI) six times, with no resulting pregnancies. Shira and Aviva paid out-of-pocket for the first three attempts, after which Shira's insurance agreed to pay for the next three attempts. The doctor who has been working with the couple has some concerns about Shira's fertility and has cautioned the couple that it is not likely that Shira will be able to conceive.

Shira and Aviva have been discussing switching to in vitro fertilization (IVF) for their next attempt at pregnancy. Shira is concerned about the degree of medical intervention that she will have to undergo in this IVF process. She does not like shots and has a high degree of stress about medical procedures. Likewise, while the couple is doing well financially, Aviva is becoming frustrated because Shira's insurance will not cover IVF for the couple—despite the insurance covering IVF for one of Shira's colleagues. Their insurance company rejected Shira and Aviva's claim because the use of donor sperm is not covered under their policy. Although the couple has put aside enough money to pay out-of-pocket for at least three rounds of IVF, Aviva is angry about the systemic discrimination in this process. Shira spoke with the insurance company about this, and the company explained that Shira's employer was responsible for negotiating the insurance plan. Shira considered discussing the issue with human resources, but an informal conversation with a friend in the department let her know that the only way to address the issue was through a grievance with the company, and Shira is not ready to take that step at this time.

Shira wants to conceive and believes that IVF is her only option, despite the low potential success rate. At the last appointment, the doctor suggested that they inseminate Aviva as they "are lucky to have two women, so might as well do what's easiest." Aviva is open to becoming pregnant yet understands that Shira would like to continue trying. Shira feels that, because she is older, she should try to become pregnant first and that, after she conceives, she would be open to Aviva trying to conceive. Shira is ashamed of feeling like she is being irrational in this process. In therapy, Shira describes being unable to voice her desires to Aviva, and she describes this as a roadblock for their physical and emotional intimacy. Shira and Aviva have had substantially less physical and sexual contact since beginning fertility treatments, although Shira appears reluctant to relate their sexual intimacy with the fertility process. Shira states that she wakes up early most days and ruminates on her situation for several hours before her alarm goes off. She is distracted while at work and unable to contribute to projects or focus. She states that she still spends time with Aviva and her friends but feels as though talking with her friends about her circumstances will be a burden to them, and she no longer is fully present when with Aviva or her friends. Shira describes feeling this anxiety increasingly over the past two months as she and Aviva have been discussing IVF.

Shira has had an intermittent history of engaging in talk therapy to support her through difficult times. She reports that previous therapists have told her she is not depressed, although sometimes she has felt similar to how she is feeling now in response to stressful life experiences.

GUIDING QUESTIONS

- What questions would you need to ask to better understand the nature of the problem?

- What individual-level medical aspects of reproduction and the fertility process would you need to know to ensure that you are not relying on your client to provide that educational piece? What would you need to know at the mezzo and macro levels?

- What social supports exist for this client? Would you consider Shira's family a source of support, strife, or other? What about Aviva's family?

- How would you interpret the role of religion in your client's life? What is the meaning your client makes of religion? What would you need to know about the Jewish culture to assist in culturally responsive treatment? How does religion function as a protective factor? In what ways could religion also hinder the client? How would you enter into these aspects of your clinical conversation?

- What instincts and biases do you bring to hearing this case? How have your own experiences shaped your views on how to work with this client?

- What would represent success in working with this client? How will you know if your treatment has been effective?

CASE FORMULATION

Generalist Formulation

Shira is a married, professional, white, culturally Jewish woman trying to conceive with her wife. At the time of this evaluation, her reported symptoms appear most consistent with the *DSM-5* diagnosis of Adjustment Disorder, with Anxiety and Depressed Mood. Criteria for anxiety disorders and depressive disorders should be ruled out, especially given that Shira does not have a firm idea about when her symptoms began. Shira has a number of supports in her life, including an emotionally strong relationship with her wife and family. Much of her fertility treatment has been covered by insurance and the remainder has not represented a financial burden to her, although Shira is understandably frustrated with the health care system. Shira has many options for adding a child to her family, including continuing IUI, moving on to IVF, coparenting a child who her partner has conceived, adopting a child, or choosing another path to parenthood that is meaningful to her. At this time, there is no need to push her to choose a pathway to parenthood soon as she has plenty of time to decide which option makes the most sense, and she is not reporting external pressures to conceive. The focus of clinical attention should be on building strengths and providing supportive therapy to Shira in her ongoing desire to achieve a pregnancy. It would be helpful to integrate services provided with health care providers who are also part of Shira's fertility treatment. Talk therapy should be paired with a referral to a psychiatrist for a medication evaluation.

Culturally Responsive and
Queer-Affirmative Formulation

Shira is a culturally Jewish, white, cisgender, able-bodied woman who identifies as a lesbian; these are identities she has had all of her adult life. Currently, she is a married, higher-earning professional who is seeking to carry a biologically related pregnancy with her wife. Based on her high level of functioning and her reluctance to ask for help, it is possible that Shira is approaching a crisis as she continues to be stressed by fertility concerns at the biological, dyadic, familial, and systemic levels. Biologically, Shira seems to feel inadequate or like a failure due to an inability to ever achieve pregnancy, and she is pressuring herself to let go of her immediate vision of family as a child who is biologically hers for whom she is the gestational carrier. The lack of culturally responsive fertility treatment is exacerbating this, as her provider appears more focused on the success of the couple at achieving pregnancy rather than the meaning Shira is giving to being able to become pregnant herself. On a dyadic level, Shira has a history of a relationship failing due to a lack of agreement on family planning, and her inability to conceive is triggering concerns about the future of her marriage and influencing her perceptions of support from her wife, Aviva. In terms of family, although Shira's parents are not pressuring her and Aviva to conceive, Shira believes that they are eager for her to do so, which is adding to her stress. This is compounded by Shira's relationship with her sister, who will likely find it easier to conceive, in part because she is in a heterosexual relationship. Shira already has a history of comparing herself to her sister and her sister's successes, and her inability to conceive is adding to Shira's feelings of inadequacy. Although her parents are trying to be supportive, their interest in becoming grandparents means that they are not acknowledging the importance Shira is giving to carrying a child versus having Aviva try to become pregnant. This is compounding Shira's perception that her lesbian identity makes her parents view her as less than her sister—on the levels of being their child, a sibling, a woman, and a lesbian. The intersection of the female and Jewish identities is also an important consideration because Judaism mandates procreation as part of the traditions. There is also systemic stress on Shira related to her insurance denials for fertility treatments, which would be covered for Shira if she was in a heterosexual relationship. Because the insurance company is contracted for the plan by Shira's workplace, the discrimination is coming from Shira's employer, which adds a power dynamic layer to Shira's experience. The discrimination is disrupting some of Shira's work dedication and performance. This is exacerbated by the expectation that Shira collaborate with colleagues who have received more substantial fertility coverage at work. Many of these colleagues are male and thus are economically advantaged already.

TREATMENT AND ACTION PLANNING

- *Case management and referrals*: Shira could benefit from brokering resources, referrals, and connections:

    - Refer to a culturally competent, LGBTQI+ specialist for fertility treatment to help the couple feel as though their medical and psychological needs are heard by the provider. Too often, fertility centers and services providers fail to clearly have LGBTQI+ affirmative representation in their materials and marketing (Johnson, 2012; Ross, Steele, & Epstein, 2006). Providers who are culturally competent and have experience with lesbian family building are likely aware of the interest these patients have in biological pregnancy above other avenues to family building, such as adoption (Goldberg & Scheib, 2015).

- Increase Shira's LGBTQI+ specific social supports. Lesbians report less support in family building than heterosexual couples (Goldberg & Smith, 2008). A referral to a local LGBTQI+ family-focused group like Rainbow Families (www.rainbowfamiliesdc.org) could help both Shira and Aviva in the process as well as networking them to culturally responsive care providers (Ross et al., 2006; Wingo, Ingraham, & Roberts, 2018). Engaging with other LGBTQI+ activity groups, like sports groups through Team DC (www .teamdc.org), or volunteering with organizations like the Rainbow History Project (www.rainbowhistory.org), would also add to Shira's support network.

- Refer to a rabbi and/or congregation who are LGBTQI+ affirming and/or an LGBTQI+ Jewish-focused support group to engage with Shira's Jewish cultural identity and increase her support network—for example, Bet Mishpachah (www .betmish.org), Keshet (www.keshetonline.org), or Keshet Ga'avah (glbtjews.org). Providers should familiarize themselves with general Jewish conduct per *Halacha* (Jewish laws and teachings) as it relates to infertility (Hirsh, 1998) as well as with models of stigma and coping related to cultural Judaism and fertility (Remennick, 2000; Shalev & Gooldin, 2006).

- Integrate complementary medicine with Shira's treatment, including evidence-supported treatments like acupuncture (MacPherson et al., 2017), massage (Field, Diego, Hernandez-Reif, Deeds, & Figueiredo, 2009), and yoga/relaxation techniques (Nekavand, Mobini, Roshandel, & Sheikhi, 2015), or less researched modalities like Reiki and energy work. Research demonstrates the importance of alternative medicine to lesbians in combination with more traditional treatments, irrespective of the demonstrated effectiveness in clinical studies (Malley & Tasker, 2008; Smith et al., 2010).

- Address the stresses of systemic-level oppression, increase empowerment, lessen isolation in discrimination, and increase sense of purpose and efficacy by connecting the client with volunteer work and LGBTQI+ activist groups—for example, Gay and Lesbian Activists Alliance (www.glaa .org), Lambda Legal (www.lambdalegal.org), Equality Federation (www.equalityfederation.org), and Family Equality Council (www.familyequality.org).

- *Individual therapy*: As the identified client, Shira is seeking supportive psychotherapy. While several could be a good fit with her needs, individual work would develop well through a combined approach of narrative and feminist work:

  - *Narrative therapy*: A narrative approach focuses on the telling/retelling of the client's story by the client herself, leading to empowerment, helping the client process her experiences, and assisting her in seeing the story through multiple perspectives (Stark, Keathley, & Nelson, 2011). Also, this work can create rituals and traditions related to fertility treatment and reproductive cycles, balancing out the otherwise-medicalized fertility processes as well as supporting clients in the case of miscarriage or other fertility loss (Burnett & Panchal, 2008). Integrating expressive elements such as art therapy can enhance treatment (Hughes & da Silva, 2011); for Shira, this could be a way to develop her own sense of identity in and beyond the fertility process, validating her in a way that she is missing in her life. Narrative techniques will also be helpful in examining the meaning Shira is giving to the many stressors in her life, such as the breakup of her first marriage, her parents' need for a grandchild, her changing relationship with Aviva, and the relationship between Shira and her workplace.

- *Feminist therapy*: Feminist and lesbian-informed therapy would focus on the unique experiences of lesbian women and a female-centered perspective (i.e., as they relate to the process of becoming a mother) (Chabot & Ames, 2004; Shapiro, 2009). Empowerment and self-efficacy are key tenets to increase Shira's feelings of control in the fertility process. Feminist and lesbian therapies consider the role of social expectations and pressures placed on Shira, and they help give voice to the roles she is taking as a professional woman, as a daughter, and as a wife, as well as her own identities and the meaning she gives them. Recognition of LGBTQI+ identities in the family-building process should be incorporated into treatment, including considering Shira taking on the pregnancy responsibilities and the less well-defined motherhood role that lesbians experience as part of their identities (Hayman, Wilkes, Halcomb, & Jackson, 2015).

- *Couples therapy*: Although the initial request for therapy was made alone by Shira, there is an indication that couples therapy would be warranted, if not prescribed. Several options of clinical theories and interventions support the couple relationship in the therapeutic process, particularly as the couple engages in family building, including the following:

  - Relational cultural theory (RCT) has been shown to strengthen LGBTQI+ couple relationships throughout the fertility process (Jordan, 2010; Rausch & Wikoff, 2017; Singh & Moss, 2016). RCT is undergirded by the assumption that a desire to be accepted by one's partner can lead an individual to diminish or hide their faults and failings. When one or both people do not give their partner the opportunity to accept their flaws, the result is an inauthentic relationship predicated on perfection. This leads to pressure to maintain the perfect self while also resulting in an unfulfilling relationship. For this couple, Shira sees her inability to become pregnant as her fault. She has tried to shield Aviva from this perception, lest Aviva also blame Shira for their lack of pregnancy and find Shira undesirable. This creates an inability for Aviva to accept Shira's perceived shortcomings, resulting in a lack of true connection between the couple. With RCT, the practitioner works to help both members of the couple learn how to accept themselves and their perceived failures and then to disclose these perceived failures within the couple, thus strengthening the relationship. For this couple, this means helping Shira face her inability to conceive a pregnancy thus far and supporting her as she shares the feelings of failure about this with Aviva. This creates the opportunity for mutual support and acceptance between Shira and Aviva, thus increasing their individual worth and couple feelings of acceptance and intimacy.

- Systemic family therapy (SFT) has been applied to LGBTQI+ families who are building a family and have experienced marginalization at the systemic level (DeDiego, 2016). In SFT, the practitioner joins with the couple or family to name, define, understand, and work through social and systemic barriers. Psychological distress in couples engaging in fertility treatment often relates to roles within the couple relationship as well as stereotypical male/female roles, couple communication, and repeating conflict cycles (Peterson, 2015; Peterson, Newton, Rosen, & Skaggs, 2006). In working with LGBTQI+ couples, pay particular attention to their beliefs about what their roles are within the relationship as well as on other system levels. For this couple, Shira's strong identity as culturally Jewish and as a daughter likely is contributing to her stress around conceiving. Also, Shira's feelings that Aviva is not hearing her could be due to Aviva's focus on problem-solving above listening (in the role of "problem solver" versus "supporter"). Helping the couple understand their implicit roles from within and outside of the couple is the first step to addressing unmet needs. The practitioner's role is also to validate systemic-level challenges, such as the medical, work, and health insurance systems. While SFT does not change these systems, acknowledging the systemic injustice the couple is experiencing validates their experience and can work to empower Shira and Aviva both within their relationship (e.g., to speak up about their needs and concerns to one another) and with greater systems in which the couple exists (e.g., to talk about the perceived stress to reproduce from their larger family system).

• *Intimacy and psychosexual functioning*: An assessment of and supportive therapy around sexual intimacy would help heal the rift in Shira and Aviva's physical relationship that began during fertility treatment. These treatments recontextualize sex through a medical model, resulting in less sexual intimacy and engagement (Nelson, Shindel, Naughton, Ohebshalom, & Mulhall, 2008; Peterson, 2015). Although Shira and Aviva are not attempting to conceive through sexual means, it is important for the practitioner to be aware of the effects their fertility process is having on their sexual functioning as a couple, particularly because many fertility treatments involve hormones that can increase or decrease a woman's sexual interest level. As the practitioner, it is part of treatment to ensure that the couple is educated about possible medically induced sexual side effects of the fertility process in addition to normalizing the psychosocial stressors that can lead to a reduction of sexual activity between members of the couple at this time.

RESOURCES

On Queer Parenting

Hermin, G. (2017). *The kids: The children of LGBTQ parents in the USA.* New York, NY: New Press.

Hicks, S. (2011). *Lesbian, gay and queer parenting: Families, intimacies, genealogies.* New York, NY: Palgrave Macmillan.

Ridd, S. (2001). *The queer parent's primer: A lesbian and gay families' guide to navigating through a straight world.* Oakland, CA: New Harbinger.

On Fertility and Becoming Parents

Borkoski, K. (2015). *Lesbian conception 101: An easy-to-follow, how-to get started guide for lesbians thinking about getting pregnant tomorrow or in a couple of years.* San Francisco, CA: Tootsie Mama.

Brill, S. (2006). *The new essential guide to lesbian conception, pregnancy, and birth.* New York, NY: Alyson Books.

Lev, A. I. (2004). *The complete lesbian and gay parenting guide.* New York, NY: Berkley.

Rosswood, E. (2016). *Journey to same-sex parenthood: Firsthand advice, tips and stories from lesbian and gay couples.* New York, NY: New Horizon.

REFERENCES

Burnett, J. A., & Panchal, K. (2008). Incorporating ideological context in counseling couples experiencing infertility. *Journal of Humanistic Counseling, Education and Development, 47*(2), 187–199.

Chabot, J. M., & Ames, B. D. (2004). "It wasn't 'let's get pregnant and go do it'": Decision making in lesbian couples planning motherhood via donor insemination. *Family Relations, 53*(4), 348–356.

DeDiego, A. C. (2016). A systemic perspective for working with same-sex parents. *Counseling Today, 59*(4), 40–44.

Field, T., Diego, M., Hernandez-Reif, M., Deeds, O., & Figueiredo, B. (2009). Pregnancy massage reduces prematurity, low birthweight and postpartum depression. *Infant Behavior and Development, 32*(4), 454–460.

Goldberg, A. E., & Scheib, J. E. (2015). Why donor insemination and not adoption? Narratives of female-partnered and single mothers. *Family Relations, 64*(5), 726–742.

Goldberg, A. E., & Smith, J. A. (2008). Social support and psychological well-being in lesbian and heterosexual pre-adoptive couples. *Family Relations, 57*(3), 281–294.

Hayman, B., Wilkes, L., Halcomb, E. J., & Jackson, D. (2015). Lesbian women choosing motherhood: The journey to conception. *Journal of GLBT Family Studies, 11*(4), 395–409.

Hirsh, A. V. (1998). Infertility in Jewish couples, biblical and rabbinic law. *Human Fertility, 1*(1), 14–19.

Hughes, E. G., & da Silva, A. M. (2011). A pilot study assessing art therapy as a mental health intervention for subfertile women. *Human Reproduction, 26*(3), 611–615.

Johnson, K. M. (2012). Excluding lesbian and single women? An analysis of U.S. fertility clinic websites. *Women's Studies International Forum, 35*(5), 394–402.

Jordan, J. V. (2017). *Relational-cultural therapy* (2nd ed.). Washington, DC: American Psychological Association.

MacPherson, H., Vickers, A., Bland, M., Torgerson, D., Corbett, M., Spackman, E., & Watt, I. (2017). Acupuncture for chronic pain and depression in primary care: A programme of research. *Programme Grants for Applied Research, 5*(3), 1–342.

Malley, M., & Tasker, F. (2008). "The difference that makes a difference": What matters to lesbians and gay men in psychotherapy. *Journal of Gay & Lesbian Psychotherapy, 11*(1–2), 93–109.

Nekavand, M., Mobini, N., Roshandel, S., & Sheikhi, A. (2015). A survey on the impact of relaxation on anxiety and the result of IVF in patients with infertility that have been referred to the infertility centers of Tehran University of Medical Sciences during 2012–2013. *Journal of Urmia Nursing and Midwifery Faculty, 13*(7), 605–612.

Nelson, C. J., Shindel, A., Naughton, C., Ohebshalom, M., & Mulhall, J. (2008). Prevalence and predictors of sexual problems, relationship stress, and depression in female partners of infertile couples. *Journal of Sexual Medicine, 5*(8), 1907–1914.

Peterson, B. (2015). Fertility counseling for couples. In S. N. Covington (Ed.), *Fertility counseling: Clinical guide and case studies* (pp. 60–73). Cambridge, UK: Cambridge University Press.

Peterson, B. D., Newton, C. R., Rosen, K. H., & Skaggs, G. E. (2006). Gender differences in how men and women who are referred for IVF cope with infertility stress. *Human Reproduction, 21*(9), 2443–2449.

Rausch, M. A., & Wikoff, H. D. (2017). Addressing concerns with lesbian couples experiencing fertility treatment: Using relational cultural theory. *Journal of LGBT Issues in Counseling, 11*(3), 142–155.

Remennick, L. (2000). Childless in the land of imperative motherhood: Stigma and coping among infertile Israeli women. *Sex Roles, 43*(11–12), 821–841.

Ross, L. E., Steele, L. S., & Epstein, R. (2006). Lesbian and bisexual women's recommendations for improving the provision of assisted reproductive technology services. *Fertility and Sterility, 86*(3), 735–738.

Shalev, C., & Gooldin, S. (2006). The uses and misuses of in vitro fertilization in Israel: Some sociological and ethical considerations. *Nashim: A Journal of Jewish Women's Studies & Gender Issues, 12*, 151–176.

Shapiro, C. H. (2009). Therapy with infertile heterosexual couples: It's not about gender—or is it? *Clinical Social Work Journal, 37*(2), 140–149.

Singh, A., & Moss, L. (2016). Using relational-cultural theory in LGBTQQ counseling: Addressing heterosexism and enhancing relational competencies. *Journal of Counseling & Development, 94*(4), 398–404.

Smith, H. A., Matthews, A., Markovic, N., Youk, A., Danielson, M. E., & Talbott, E. O. (2010). A comparative study of complementary and alternative medicine use among heterosexually and lesbian identified women: Data from the ESTHER project. *Journal of Alternative and Complementary Medicine, 16*(11), 1161–1170.

Stark, M. D., Keathley, R. S., & Nelson, J. A. (2011). A developmental model for counseling infertile couples. *The Family Journal, 19*(2), 225–230.

Wingo, E., Ingraham, N., & Roberts, S. C. M. (2018). Reproductive health care priorities and barriers to effective care for LGBTQ people assigned female at birth: A qualitative study. *Women's Health Issues, 28*(4), 350–357.

5

THE COLLEAGUE

PAM BOWERS

You are beginning your second semester as a social work intern at a local drop-in center for homeless families. The agency is relatively small with an executive director, a grants/budget analyst, a lead social worker, two AmeriCorps volunteers, and an administrative support staff person. The agency is located in a small rural community in the Midwest with a regional population under 60,000 people. This is the kind of community where it is easy to run into your neighbors, classmates, and coworkers when you are eating at a restaurant or shopping for groceries.

Last semester when you began the internship, you became friends with Taylor, who is the administrative support staff person. Taylor is a nineteen-year-old Jewish, transgender man who lives with his parents. Taylor has a close relationship with his mom as they spend a lot of time together and share a love for reading. Taylor is less close to his dad, who is often away from home working two jobs and only around for religious holidays and some weekends when he gets a break. Last year, Taylor began to publicly identify as a male and has since been focusing on his physical and public transition (from female to male). He told you he applied for the position at the agency to save money to buy a car and move out to live in a bigger city. Taylor knows the bigger city has more support programs for transgender and other gender-diverse people, as well as doctors willing to pre-scribe hormone replacement therapy for people transitioning and confirming their gender. Taylor's current gender transition, in-cluding using male-identified pronouns (e.g., "he" and "him") and wearing more masculine clothing, is unknown to most of his other family and former high school classmates in the com-munity. Still, Taylor's parents are generally supportive of his gen-der transition.

Many people in the community knew Taylor as a tomboy growing up; he discloses that he often experienced homophobic harassment from people who thought he was a lesbian. Taylor has been very isolated since his early teens and often stays home to read and browse Internet videos. When he goes out in the community, it is mostly to go to the gym or to work. He claims that people generally leave him alone and he often does not en-gage in any small talk with old acquaintances. This job is his first where he has experienced more encounters with the public, including homeless individuals and families, some of whom he recognizes. He feels that people do not make many comments about his changed appearance because he feels they may be em-barrassed that he sees them in a space seeking help and resources for housing and employment.

Taylor began his transition after being hired at the agency; thus, Taylor was initially known as female with she/her pronouns among coworkers and drop-in center clients. He said he made a point to meet with the executive director to tell her about this change and his preferred pronouns and requests to use the men's restroom. Throughout his transition over the past three months, he has run into several issues within the agency; in addition, you have observed some of them and heard some of his stories when you two talk. For example, despite his gender identity and gender presentation, the executive director keeps using female pronouns for Taylor such as "she filed the paper work" or "she's going to make that order for us." Unfortunately, the executive director often does not apologize for the mistake or even recognize that one has been made, which leaves Taylor to feel uncomfortable and embarrassed. Taylor has also been told by the executive director that he must use the restroom congruent with his sex assigned at birth, especially because she fears Taylor may confuse the clients who share the same restroom with staff. This means that Taylor, who was born female but identifies and presents as male, must continue to use the women's restroom at his place of employment. He feels extremely uncomfortable using the women's restroom, so instead of using the restroom at work, Taylor waits over eight hours until he gets home from work to use the bathroom or will often spend his extra money to go out to lunch or purchase coffee somewhere so he can use a men's restroom.

The executive director said to Taylor that, until he has his gender legally changed and reflected on his personnel file, he will continue to be required to use the women's restroom. There are no other nondiscrimination policies in the agency that he can reference, so the word of the executive director is what goes. In your state, the requirement for a legal gender change requires a letter from a medical provider confirming appropriate clinical treatment for gender transition, which may include surgical procedures and a court order to change the birth certificate. Unfortunately, because you live in a rural community, the wait list to see the one doctor in a nearby county, who has been rumored to support people seeking gender transition, is over nine months long.

Since returning to your internship this semester, Taylor has been more withdrawn when you try to say hello or text him to see how things are going. He generally seems depressed, and you sense he is anxious about the demands of the executive director, including being required to use the women's restroom. He may be keeping his head down because he is working so hard to save money to leave town and would rather not push the executive director even if it means not being accepted by her as his authentic self. You have also noticed that the executive director has been very short with Taylor in simple interactions, almost as if she is avoiding any personal contact with him. Taylor, however, has continued to be very friendly with drop-in center clients. After making these observations, you have decided you want to help Taylor by advocating for policy change and generally increasing awareness at the agency about issues facing transgender employees, clients, and community members. However, you are not sure what that will mean in terms of keeping your internship placement secured. You are just one semester from graduating, and you are concerned that the executive director, who is your supervisor for the internship, will not have a favorable response.

GUIDING QUESTIONS

- As a student intern, what are your responsibilities, if any, to address the issues presented? Taylor is clearly *not* your client; still, what are your ethical obligations? How might your own moral imperatives/values figure into this case?
- Considering Taylor as the person directly affected in this case, how might you approach addressing your own concerns/ethical responsibilities while considering Taylor in the situation?
- Which social work competencies and ethical standards provide guidance on the best way to address the issues presented? How might you specifically incorporate that guidance as a social work intern?

- If Taylor were your client, what would you advise? How would your ethical obligations and imperatives in treatment change? What information provided in this case would you use to develop a treatment plan?
- Which agency, municipal/county, state, and national policies may support and/or hinder progress for Taylor?

CASE FORMULATION

Generalist Formulation

Taylor recently came out at work as male where his coworkers previously knew him as female. He is experiencing distress about equal treatment at work based on his gender identity, including lack of access to the bathroom that matches his gender identity. He wants to keep his job so he can save money to buy a car and move to a bigger city, and most likely he would have a hard time finding similar work elsewhere in this rural community.

Culturally Responsive and Queer-Affirmative Formulation

Taylor is a newly out transgender, Jewish nineteen-year-old who is facing several issues related to living in a rural area and working in a small nonprofit agency. He will not be able to schedule a medical appointment with the only doctor in the area who can assist with gender transitioning for a minimum of nine months. In addition, he is facing the tough decision to stay at his job to save money for his goal of moving to a bigger city with medical and support resources or to quit the job and be in less distress due to the issues he is facing at work. The agency has no clear policy on nondiscrimination based on gender identity; however, the executive director has been firm in her decision to discriminate based on gender identity. The social work intern believes they have an ethical duty in this situation and would like to advocate for Taylor as well as transgender-inclusive policies within the agency but is experiencing internal conflict regarding their role as a student.

TREATMENT AND ACTION PLANNING

- *Role of the intern*: The social work intern has a unique opportunity to educate the agency about supporting transgender employees and clients. The intern could engage in a variety of discussions to advance more equitable policies and a culturally responsive work setting:

  - With the executive director (who is also the intern's supervisor), discuss the intern's concerns to the supervisor, who may or may not be receptive of the information.
  - With Taylor, identify alternative ways to advocate for and support Taylor that may not require support or permission from the executive director. Also, collaborate with Taylor in discussion and action planning to promote mutual respect, self-determination, and Taylor's empowerment.
  - With the intern's social work program, engage the field director and/or field liaison in processing personal, professional, and ethical considerations. In addition, discuss the potential roles the university may play in this agency as well as the larger community. Should the university step in when a student may

be in a potentially harmful placement? What if the student were transgender; would this situation be different?

- *Engaged activities*: The intern can engage in a variety of pragmatic exercises to work through the issues at hand. This could be done in a field seminar or other practice-based course. For example, the intern could harness a macro-oriented perspective and engage in a power-mapping activity to address the key players, relevant policies (and model examples), and other related agencies in the rural context that may have existing policies. Similarly, they could identify professional development learning opportunities and/or mentors to prepare to address this issue. Given the rural context, the intern appreciates that relationships are key and important to such a practice environment. Therefore, an opportunity exists to create or fracture positive lasting relationships for future employment. Being prepared in advance will have long-term impacts.

RESOURCES

Educational resources for transgender and gender non-conforming students: www2.ed.gov/about/offices/list/ocr/lgbt.html

National Center for Transgender Equality: transequality.org

Trans employment program employer services: transemploymentprogram.org/employers

U.S. Equal Employment Opportunity Commission and enforcement protections for LGBT workers: www.eeoc.gov/eeoc/newsroom/wysk/enforcement_protections_lgbt_workers.cfm

REFERENCES

Austin, A., Craig, S. L., Alessi, E. J., Wagaman, M. A., Paceley, M. S., Dziengel, L., & Balestryer, J. E. (2016). *Guidelines for transgender and gender nonconforming (TGNC) affirmative education: Enhancing the climate for TGNC students, staff and faculty in social work education.* Alexandria, VA: Council on Social Work Education.

Bender-Baird, K. (2011). *Transgender employment experiences: Gendered perceptions and the law.* Albany: State University of New York Press.

Morrow, D. F., & Messinger, L. (Eds.). (2006). *Sexual orientation and gender expression in social work practice: Working with gay, lesbian, bisexual, and transgender people.* New York, NY: Columbia University Press.

Russell, A. C. (2013). Building community among rural gay, lesbian, bisexual, and transgender persons: Connecting community through families of choice. In T. L. Scales, C. L. Streeter, & H. S. Cooper (Eds.), *Rural social work: Building and sustaining community capacity* (pp. 99–111). Hoboken, NJ: John Wiley.

Vade, D. (2005). Expanding gender and expanding the law: Toward a social and legal conceptualization of gender that is more inclusive of transgender people. *Michigan Journal of Gender and Law, 11*(2), 252–316.

Weil, M. (2013). *The handbook of community practice.* Thousand Oaks, CA: Sage.

6

DOWN BUT NOT OUT

GITA R. MEHROTRA, MEG PANICHELLI,

AND STEPH NG PING CHEUNG

B is a twenty-eight-year-old Taiwanese immigrant who identifies as a nonbinary femme (using they/them pronouns) who has been in the United States for about two years on a student visa. They are attending a large state university and are still undecided about their major. B currently lives with their partner, L, a white, U.S. citizen, cisgender woman who identifies as a lesbian. B has a somewhat distant relationship with their family back home in Taiwan but has some connection to an aunt and uncle who have been living in the United States for many years. B decided to come to the United States in part so that they could gain some distance from their immediate family to more freely explore their gender identity and sexual orientation. Having some family in the United States made it somewhat easier to convince their parents that they would be okay in the United States, and going to school and getting a student visa felt like one way to emigrate from Taiwan. B did not date much in Taiwan but has been questioning their gender identity and sexual orientation since they were a young teenager.

B's partnership to L is their first romantic queer relationship, and L is the first romantic partner with whom B has lived. They first met at a local queer bar and were instantly attracted to one another. B loved to go dancing with friends there every weekend; L was captivated by their outgoing personality. Since they started dating, L always paid for everything and made B feel taken care of and safe. After a few months of living together, however, their relationship started to feel different to B. L started getting upset when B made evening plans without her and often expressed disapproval of how much time B spent with their friends. She became particularly jealous of the relationships B had with other Taiwanese students on campus and did not like it when B would speak Mandarin to their friends and family. B currently has a limited income as they are getting some money from a work study job on campus and some money that their family periodically sends them from Taiwan. Because of their visa status, their employment opportunities are limited, and they have considered exploring other under-the-table options to increase their income.

During the first year of their relationship, there were a few times when arguments escalated between B and L. For example, one evening a few months ago while attending a queer dance party together, L yelled and grabbed at B, accusing them of cheating on her by dancing with their other friends at the bar. B shoved L back, and L fell and hit her head, which resulted in some minor cuts and bruising. When they got home that night, L locked B in their bedroom to give them time to think about how they embarrassed her. In the morning, L apologized and promised that she would not do that again; she just loved B so much that she did not want them to make bad choices. L often says she is the only one who truly knows B and that no one else would love them like her.

Three months ago, after they had been dating for a year, L proposed to B, assuring them that marriage would be good for their relationship; moreover, it would be helpful for B to apply for a green card, as their student visa would expire soon. B loves L and so said yes but is not sure if she is really the one. L has started pressuring B to come out to their family and friends at school so that they can publicly celebrate their engagement. Arguments often ensue as B feels coming out will only add more strain and distance with their family. Since the proposal, L has been getting increasingly violent, hitting and kicking B. L apologizes often and promises she is trying to be better, all the while contending that B often provokes her to anger.

Over the past six weeks, B has been experiencing a growing intensity with episodic depression and consistent periods of disruptive and irregular sleep patterns. B increasingly disassociates from their body during sex. B would like to potentially pursue hormone replacement therapy and get hip pads and breast forms to feel more comfortable in their body. L says that she thinks any medical transition is a bad idea and that she likes B the way they are.

Last night, B refused to have sex with L, and L repeatedly punched and choked B until they passed out. B woke up to the bedroom door being locked again, while L had gone to work, and B climbed down from their second-story apartment window. B feels like they cannot take it anymore and have nowhere to go as they are not out to their aunt and uncle and most of their friends. They also do not feel safe telling their small group of queer friends about what is going on because L is well liked in their friendship group and they are worried they will not be believed and also do not want to ruin L's reputation. They remember being at the bar and noticing a flyer about a domestic violence (DV) agency in their neighborhood, and they decided to contact the organization to see if anyone could help them.

GUIDING QUESTIONS

- What would be priority areas to explore, assess, and on which to take action?

- What theories, models, and approaches might be useful for understanding this case?

- What about this case fits with our assumptions about domestic violence? Does this case challenge our assumptions about domestic violence? If so, how?

- What considerations might be helpful when thinking about the role of alcohol and other drug use in dynamics between B and L? How about the role of race/racism and citizenship? Transphobia?

- What questions might you ask to assess B's sense of safety, support, and agency in their current circumstances?

- If B were to contact you and asked what they could do differently so that L would stop being abusive, how might you respond? What additional questions might you ask to assess the power and control dynamics in the relationship?

- How might you start the conversation to engage B in processing their DV-related trauma?

- What are your own biases and insecurities that this case study evokes? What will you need to overcome them?

CASE FORMULATION

Generalist Formulation

B, a twenty-eight-year-old transgender immigrant from Taiwan, is engaged to L, who is a white woman, a U.S. citizen, and a lesbian who has never dated a trans or nonbinary person before.

Over the two years of their relationship, L's deployment of power and control tactics has escalated and most recently includes sexually assaulting B and choking them until they passed out. Although B sometimes fears for their life and currently feels as though they cannot take the abuse anymore, they are afraid of the consequences of leaving L. B lives with L, is quite isolated, has a limited income, and does not have other housing options. L has also recently been threatening to "out" B to their family in the United States, which is extremely distressing for B (Lindhorst, mehrotra, & Mincer, 2009; Nascimento & Scorsolini-Comin, 2018). Once B finishes school, their student immigration status will expire, and without marrying L, B fears that the process toward U.S. citizenship will be completely inaccessible.

In fact, B's precarious citizenship status makes this their top concern, especially given the conservative, anti-immigrant political climate in which immigrants are under siege as well as the ongoing threats regarding immigration enforcement in the United States. In addition, B experiences episodic depression and disruptive sleep patterns. B is in need of safety, resources, and support, including possibly accessing a DV shelter.

Culturally Responsive and Queer-Affirmative Formulation

Building beyond singular attention to the dynamic of violence and control, we must also recognize how B's intersecting identities are inextricable from their relationship, experience of abuse, and love for L (Kanuha, 2013; Pusey & mehrotra, 2011). L is B's first true love and first queer relationship. B lives in the United States, separate from their parents and extended family; they are an only child. They also have limited social support outside of their community of Taiwanese friends at school, and they feel isolated from many sources of comfort for them. All the while, their relationship with L has been a significant part of their sense of family in the United States. B's isolation has been compounded by being in this abusive relationship with L. This lack of a support network may limit options around what safety can and will look like for B as they make decisions around leaving their relationship and accessing services. L consistently reminds B that once their student visa expires and people find out they are in the United States and undocumented, they could risk deportation, which would not happen if they were married. B fears what will happen if L outs them to their family and to immigration officials, even if those threats do not come to fruition. B may feel safer and more informed about their options and resources if they had access to services in Mandarin with advocates who are queer, trans, or queer/trans affirmative and who can identify with the intersections of migration and homophobia/transphobia among Asian and Pacific Islander (API), Chinese, or Taiwanese family members (Kanuha, 2013).

Furthermore, from an intersectional feminist perspective (Collins, 2000; Crenshaw, 1991; de Vries, 2015; mehrotra, 2010), B faces the interconnectedness of oppressions targeted at their marginalized social locations in addition to the complexities of experiencing abuse in their relationship (Pusey & mehrotra, 2011). As a recent immigrant from Taiwan with a student visa, a nonbinary femme queer, and a person with mental health struggles, B must also navigate systemic barriers created by the overlapping and intersecting effects of ethnocentrism, racism, xenophobia, cissexism, transphobia, sexism, heterosexism, and ableism (Asian Pacific Institute on Gender-Based Violence, 2018). These might include fear of criminal and/or immigration system involvement if immigrant status is disclosed; refusal of medical services based on trans/homophobia in health care toward queer, trans, and nonbinary people; disbelief that intimate partner violence occurs in queer relationships (Ristock & Timbang, 2005); discrimination and alienation within mainstream shelters for survivors of domestic violence; potential language barriers; impatience; and improper diagnoses by mental health practitioners, among many other barriers that may arise. The intersections of B's identities also shape the concept of what "culturally responsive resources" would look like for B. The ability to access such culturally responsive services will also be influenced by where they are geographically in the United States; for example, if they are in San Francisco, there is a large, if not the largest, Chinese community (outside of China and Taiwan) and sizable queer and Chinese, Taiwanese, or API communities as well as attendant social and health services. Alternatively, outside a community with that sort of concentration of communities, B faces the daunting proposition of attempting to access services that may or may not exist—but moreover would inherently not be organized with representation and responsiveness.

TREATMENT AND ACTION PLANNING

■ *Safety planning:* B needs to address immediate safety concerns and increase their safety; these conversations and action would include the following:

- Brainstorming with B about ways to increase their safety without necessarily using police or other systems such as using friend networks; this may include a discussion of what safety means and looks like for them in the current moment (Burk, Al-Aswad Dillsi, & Crager, 2013; Creative Interventions, 2012; Pusey & mehrotra, 2011), as well as safety planning for day-to-day survival given that they may be staying in their shared housing with L for some time while determining other options (FORGE, 2013).

- Helping B to determine what important documents they need to keep with them in case of an emergency or needing to leave town and/or the country (FORGE, 2013)
- Exploring community accountability options with B—specifically exploring if there may be ways for L's friends and peer network to hold L accountable for her abusive behavior (Creative Interventions, 2012; INCITE!, 2003; Pusey & mehrotra, 2011)

■ *Case management*: B is in need of various resource/referrals and advocacy to meet basic needs and access relevant services:

- Look into options for domestic violence shelters or other transitional housing possibilities that are gender inclusive. As more and more shelters are offering space to people of all genders, it would be helpful to identify viable options for B if they decide to leave (FORGE, 2016).
- Assess health care needs and insurance options, including mental health resources and interventions as well as gender-affirming health care options (e.g., hormone replacement therapy).
- Provide access to affirming domestic violence community programs and, specifically, support groups for queer and trans survivors of violence (GLBTQ Domestic Violence Project, 2016).
- Obtain resources for gender-affirming items such as clothing, makeup, hip pads, and so on.

■ *Trauma-informed care*: It is important that B is able to meet other queer and/or trans Asian immigrant survivors of abuse

(Pusey & mehrotra, 2011). Due to the complex trauma B has experienced, including the domestic violence from L, as well as the trauma of experiencing ongoing oppression (as a queer and trans Asian immigrant living in the United States) and migration, they are in need of culturally responsive trauma-informed support, validation, and education related to the violence they have been surviving in their relationship.

- *Affirming and accessible health care*: B will need access to cultur-ally responsive and gender-affirming health care so that they can explore hormone therapy and access other medical and mental health care as needed. In addition, given B's cultural background, it is not clear what kind of meaning making they make around depression and anxiety or suicidality, but this will need to be explored further moving forward.
- *Housing advocacy*: B needs to obtain affordable, safe, long-term housing. If B is living in a major metropolitan area, housing options that are affordable to B may be limited as the housing market is shaped by gentrification and lack of access, especially for B, who has limited income and a short rental history in the United States. Still, this is a significant need for B, as they will need to obtain safe housing to separate from L. B also has limited financial options and income given their student visa status. B may not want to seek shelter in the mainstream DV service system given that most services are based on the gender binary, and B may experience transpho-bia from service providers as well as other shelter residents. This work includes the following:

  - Assess B's financial situation, including current sources of income and if they have access to that income, family sup-port, and so on.
  - Identify housing resources within existing community net-works (e.g., sublet options and/or private landlord where

there are potentially fewer formal hurdles such as application and screening fees, shared housing, etc.).

- Look into emergency housing options as well as other resources such as basic food items through B's university.
- Support B with consistent safety planning while working with B toward finding their own housing as that may include staying with L longer than may be desired.

■ *Immigration support*: B needs legal support regarding their options for staying in the United States. Their immigration status is of significant concern, given the current political climate (toward immigrants), their strong desire to stay in the United States, the current time-limited student visa, and a relative lack of options for obtaining longer-term legal status. B is also stressed about money and has limited options for increasing their income. This work includes the following:

- Using the Transgender Law Center Trans Immigrant Defense Effort to gain further information about legal issues or concerns related to immigration (https://transgenderlawcenter .org/programs/tide)
- Identifying and consulting with an immigration attorney who is also familiar with LGBTQ+ issues and LGBTQ+ specific petitions
- Consulting with the International Student Office within B's university regarding visa options and potentially supporting B to meet with their advisor for further support

■ *Committed action*: B has expressed interest in staying connected to the Taiwanese community at their university as well as building more LGBTQ+ friends and community. Over the course of their relationship, L has isolated B from their

Taiwanese friends at school, which may make turning to them for support at this time difficult. B's family and Taiwanese friends are not queer, and B is concerned that they will not be queer affirming. If B has friends and community who are non-API queers, they may not necessarily understand the ways that racism, xenophobia, and immigration processes affect B's particular experience. This type of work includes the following:

- Explore local queer resources to find opportunities to connect with queer communities such as LGBTQ+ resource centers, queer and trans people of color events, and so on.
- Identify other avenues for building more social networks around shared interests, shared values, and shared identities, such as dancing, meet-ups, book groups, and LGBTQ+ healthy relationships workshops, among other avenues.
- Connect with culturally specific queer groups, such as the National Queer Asian Pacific Islander Alliance (www.nq apia.org) and other local or regional queer API groups.
- Continue involvement with Taiwanese friends and cultural groups at their university. Begin to discuss and strategize about coming out to more Taiwanese friends, including finding culturally relevant resources for allies and helping B to identify a process for building more support in existing relationships with a Taiwanese friend group (National Education Association, n.d.).

RESOURCES

FORGE: https://forge-forward.org/
National Domestic Violence Hotline. (n.d.). LGBT power and control wheel. Retrieved from https://www.thehotline.org/is-this-abuse/lgbt -abuse/lgbt-power-and-control-wheel/
The Network/La Red: http://tnlr.org/en/

New York City Anti-Violence Project. (2017). Lesbian, gay, bisexual, transgender, and HIV-affected intimate partner violence in 2016: A report from the national coalition of anti-violence programs; 2017 release edition. Retrieved from https://avp.org/LGBTQ+-ipv-2016/

The Northwest Network: https://www.nwnetwork.org/

Stanton, M., Rozas, L., & Asencio, M. (2018). Citizenship status matters: A social factor influencing outness among a diverse national sample of LGBT individuals. *British Journal of Social Work.* Retrieved from https://doi.org/10.1093/bjsw/bcy079

Transgender Law Center: https://transgenderlawcenter.org/

REFERENCES

Asian Pacific Institute on Gender-Based Violence. (2018). Directory of domestic & gender violence serving Asians and Pacific Islanders. Retrieved from http://apiidv.org/resources/directory-api-services/

Burk, C., Al-Aswad Dillsi, S., & Crager, M. (2013). *It takes a village, people! Advocacy, friends, and family & LGBT survivors of abuse.* Retrieved from https://static1.squarespace.com/static/566c7f0c2399a3bdabb57553/t/566c9be29cadb6bf7efc8e1e/1449958370563/It-Takes-A-Village-People-Web-Version.pdf

Collins, P. H. (2000). *Black feminist thought: Knowledge, consciousness, and the politics of empowerment.* New York, NY: Routledge.

Creative Interventions. (2012). Creative Interventions toolkit: A practical guide to stop interpersonal violence. Retrieved from http://www.creative-interventions.org/tools/toolkit/

Crenshaw, K. (1991). Mapping the margins: Intersectionality, identity politics, and violence against women of color. *Stanford Law Review, 43*(6), 1241–1299.

de Vries, K. M. (2015). Transgender people of color at the center: Conceptualizing a new intersectional model. *Ethnicities, 15*(1), 3–27.

FORGE. (2013). Safety planning: A guide for transgender and gender nonconforming individuals who are experiencing intimate partner violence. Retrieved from http://forge-forward.org/wp-content/docs/safety-planning-tool.pdf

FORGE. (2016). Gender-integrated shelters: Experience and advice. Retrieved from http://forge-forward.org/wp-content/docs/gender-integrated-shelter-interivews-FINAL.pdf

GLBTQ Domestic Violence Program. (2016). Trauma-informed approaches for LGBQT* survivors of intimate partner violence. Retrieved from https://vawnet.org/sc/organizations-focused-dv-LGBTQ+-communities

INCITE! (2003). Community accountability working document. Retrieved from https://incite-national.org/community-accountability-working -document/

Kanuha, V. K. (2013). "Relationships so loving and so hurtful": The constructed duality of sexual and racial/ethnic intimacy in the context of violence in Asian and Pacific Islander lesbian and queer women's relationships. *Violence Against Women, 19*(9), 1175–1196.

Lindhorst, T., mehrotra, G., & Mincer, S. (2009). Outing the abuse: Considerations for effective practice with lesbian, gay, bisexual and transgender survivors of intimate partner violence. In F. Danis & L. Lockhart (Eds.), *Domestic violence mosaic: Culturally competent practice with diverse populations* (pp. 232–267). New York, NY: Columbia University Press.

mehrotra, G. (2010). Toward a continuum of intersectionality theorizing for feminist social work scholarship. *Affilia, 25*(4), 417–430.

Nascimento, G., & Scorsolini-Comin, F. (2018). Revealing one's homosexuality to the family: An integrative review of the scientific literature. *Temas Em Psicologia, 26*(3), 1543–1556.

National Education Association. (n.d.). 10 things to know about LGBTQ+ API communities. Retrieved from https://www.nea.org/assets/docs /10%20Things%20to%20Know%20About%20LGBTQ+%20API%20 Communities_FinalRev1.pdf

Pusey, O., & mehrotra, g. (2011). Movement building starts with healthy relationships: Transforming silence into action in API LGBT communities. In L. Samarasinha, J. Dulani, & C. Chen (Eds.), *The revolution starts at home: Partner abuse in activist communities* (pp. 237–264). New York, NY: South End Press.

Ristock, J., & Timbang, N. (2005). Relationship violence in lesbian/gay/ bisexual/transgender/queer [LGBTQ+] communities. *Violence Against Women Online Resources.* Retrieved from http://citeseerx.ist.psu.edu /viewdoc/download?doi=10.1.1.208.7282&rep=rep1&type=pdf

7

FOSTERING, FORCING CHOICE

RICHARD A. BRANDON-FRIEDMAN

Jackie is a sixteen-year-old, African American transgender female. Jackie entered the foster care system at age five after she and her siblings were removed from her mother's care due to substantiated neglect. Jackie's mother was heavily involved with opioid use, and she had largely left the children to care for themselves. Jackie is the oldest of five children, although she has no contact with any of the siblings for whom she used to care. Department of Child Services' records indicate that Jackie began expressing herself as female around age eight, has outwardly identified as female for several years, and insists that people call her by her chosen female name.

Emotionally and socially, Jackie has had difficulties throughout her life. From an early age, she was identified as having "behavioral problems" and has a long list of mental health diagnoses, including those related to issues of conduct, mood, mania, traumatic stress, and gender, indicative of a lengthy history of involvement with social service agencies. Her most recent diagnosis, Unspecified Paraphilic Disorder, was given to her by a court-appointed assessment worker after the third time she was found engaging in oral sex with older men she met online.

Jackie's behavioral concerns have led to significant instability in her life and repeated placement changes. Prior foster parents have reported extreme disrespect, defiance, verbal aggression, argumentativeness, emotional instability, threatening behaviors, hypersensitivity, and theft. Educationally, Jackie receives special education services under the classification of having an emotional disability. Currently, she attends an alternative school housed at a local residential treatment facility. Jackie has also been involved in the legal system for several years and was recently detained for a two-week period after an incident at school.

Despite her struggles, Jackie maintained the most recent foster placement with an elderly grandmother for close to a year. The grandmother, referred to as "Granny" by Jackie, has had Jackie in her home several times over the years. Several placements in the home have been disrupted after behavioral blow-ups, but Granny took Jackie back on-and-off when other placements could not be found. Granny reported a special affinity toward Jackie, saying she sees a very vulnerable person under Jackie's hard exterior and feels Jackie could do better if Jackie would allow someone to help her. Granny has been supportive of Jackie's gender identity, saying she does not care what Jackie calls herself or how she dresses as long as she does better in life. Granny's children have concerns about Jackie's treatment of their mother and are often very critical of Jackie. Jackie reported they mock her gender expression, although Granny tries to minimize that.

Socially, Jackie presents largely as female, wearing dresses when possible. Her school has not been supportive of her, but she dresses as she pleases when around others from the foster care agency. During a recent picnic, Jackie was a star basketball player while wearing a skirt and carrying a purse on the court. All of the agency's staff and Jackie's service providers use female pronouns as Jackie requests.

Seven months ago, Jackie left Granny's house after a particularly explosive episode. The agency staff struggled with locating a possible placement due to Jackie's behavioral history and the widespread refusal of foster parents to accept an individual who identifies as transgender. While the agency staff have never spoken with Jackie directly about this reason for placement difficulties, they are aware that Jackie knows her gender identity is considered problematic by many foster parents. Jackie spent three weeks in an emergency shelter (placed with males) before the foster care agency was able to find a prospective placement with an African American family. Prior to her current placement, the agency staff met with the prospective foster parents repeatedly to discuss Jackie's behaviors as well as her gender identity. The staff insisted the family be willing to accept Jackie's female identity and allow her to live as her authentic self, which the family agreed to do.

During the past several months, Jackie's therapist has noticed that Jackie is no longer wearing female clothes. She continues to insist that the agency staff use female pronouns, but in the therapist's conversations with the foster parents, it has become clear they refer to Jackie using male pronouns exclusively. Exploring this further, Jackie admitted that the foster family had discarded all her female clothes and insists she present as male in the home, socially, and during regular attendance at weekly church-sponsored events. When the therapist raised concerns about this, Jackie became angry, accusing him of trying to sabotage her first really positive placement. Jackie then stated that if she were removed from the current foster home, she would run away back to them.

During an emergency treatment team staffing, service providers expressed similar concerns about the foster parents' response to Jackie's gender identity but also admitted Jackie was doing better than she had ever done before. She was not having any major behavioral concerns at school or in the home, and she seemed to be functioning well, socially and emotionally. Team members acknowledged that Jackie had been more cooperative in the past two months, even as she continued to insist that they use female pronouns.

GUIDING QUESTIONS

- What further information do you feel would be necessary to understand Jackie's experience of her gender identity?
- At what point does professional judgment outweigh the principle of self-determination, if ever?
- What questions would you ask when meeting with Jackie to understand her decision-making process regarding her desire to stay with the current family?
- How would you structure the conversation with the current foster family to address the concerns of the treatment team? How would you address their possible resistance or outright rejection?
- How do you decide which aspects of Jackie's trauma history should be dealt with first, that of her childhood or that related to her gender identity?

CASE FORMULATION

Generalist Formulation

Jackie has been involved with social services for much of her life due to significant behavioral and emotional difficulties. She has a history of trauma due to early neglect, for which she has been receiving therapeutic services. During the past six months,

Jackie's behavioral concerns have abated to a large degree, and her emotional regulation has increased. She has been more cooperative with service providers, possibly contributing to the improvements in her psychosocial functioning. There have been concerns in the past regarding her gender identity and gender expression, but she appears to have reached a point in which this is no longer creating difficulties in her life. Jackie has made it clear that she desires to stay in her current placement, and the service team members should accept that.

Culturally Responsive and Queer-Affirmative Formulation

Jackie is an adolescent transgender female who has experienced significant trauma in her life related to early neglect but also due to her gender identity. She has had behavioral and emotional difficulties throughout her life, some of which may be directly attributable to her struggling to understand her gender identity and others' reactions to that identity. While Jackie has been receiving social services throughout her life and her providers appear to have been supportive of her gender identity, it is not clear that her struggles with coming to terms with that identity or the social ramifications of that identity have been addressed in a therapeutic setting. Furthermore, it is necessary to explore the roles that Jackie's and the foster family's racial and religious/spiritual background/culture play in their beliefs about and level of acceptance of individuals who identify as transgender.

Even within the foster care system, Jackie has continued to experience alienation and stigmatization from foster parents and from the staff at the emergency shelter. These experiences have further exacerbated Jackie's emotional difficulties, as her gender identity is invalidated. After being told she was going to be placed in a supportive house, she instead found herself being forced to choose between her gender identity and a stable and emotionally supportive environment. The current reduction in behavioral and emotional symptomology is promising and may be used to further treatment, but there needs to be a focus on working with Jackie to understand her gender identity.

FURTHER POLICY INTERSECTIONS

The National Association of Social Workers (NASW) provides the following policy guidance (NASW, 2015, pp. 303–310):

- NASW asserts that discrimination and prejudice directed against any individuals on the basis of gender identity or gender expression, whether real or perceived, are damaging to the social, emotional, psychological, physical, and economic well-being of the affected individuals, as well as society as a whole, and NASW seeks the elimination of the same both inside and outside the profession, in public and private sectors.

- NASW encourages all institutions that train or employ social workers to broaden any nondiscriminatory statement made to students, faculty, staff, or clients, to include "gender identity or expression," in all nondiscrimination statements.

- NASW encourages the development of programs, training, and information that promote proactive efforts to eliminate psychological, social, and physical harm directed toward transgender people and to portray them accurately and compassionately.

- NASW advocates for the availability of comprehensive psychological and social support services for transgender people and their families that are respectful and sensitive to individual concerns.

TREATMENT AND ACTION PLANNING

- *Supporting and promoting gender identity and expression*: It is important to address concerns related to Jackie's gender and expression, intra- and interpersonally. This would involve a variety of steps, including the following:

  - Refer Jackie to a social worker who specializes in therapeutic work with adolescents who identify as transgender.
  - Discuss the reasons for service providers' concerns and effective ways to partner with allies and to advocate for oneself.
  - Provide possible additional education on gender identity development.
  - Assist Jackie with determining her progress in developing her gender identity and what further progress she desires (see Testa, Coolhart, & Peta, 2015).
  - Work with Jackie on understanding and coping with social and environmental stigma related to her gender identity, including within the child welfare system.
  - Assist Jackie with the development of a plan for how to deal with stigmatization and harassment in the future.
  - Process Jackie's conflict between her desire for a stable living situation and living as her authentic self.
  - Ensure Jackie has access to support or social groups for youth who identify as transgender (either in person or virtually).

- *Traumatic stress*: Up to this point, it appears that Jackie's history of trauma, on multiple levels, has not been addressed or even acknowledged. From a trauma-informed and gender-affirming approach, it is important to tend to these issues as way of ruling out issues or bringing increasing resolution and foregrounding resiliency. This approach could involve various elements, including the following:

- Provide psychoeducation regarding trauma and its effects on individuals.
- Highlight how events can be traumatic, such as stigmatization based on gender identity.
- Assist Jackie with processing emotions related to difficulties finding a foster placement for her due to her gender identity.
- Work with Jackie to explore her history of trauma using an evidence-based practice such as trauma-focused cognitive behavioral therapy (Cohen, Mannarino, & Deblinger, 2017).

■ *Foster family and system*: It is imperative to address the numerous concerns related to the foster parents' actions directly, as noted by multiple service providers. It would be important to have a frank dialogue to explain the reasons for service providers' concerns, to inform foster parents of agency standards for care for youth, and to ensure foster parents understand what is required of them.

■ *Stigma*: Related to the point above, it would be necessary to address the process of stigmatization and the probable deficits in cultural awareness among foster parents, as related to youth who identify as transgender. Presuming that the foster parents are receptive, the social worker would need to provide psycho-education on what gender identity entails and what it means to identify as transgender. In addition, the foster parents can be provided with information to counteract their stereotypes and prejudices regarding individuals who identify as transgender. As well, the social worker would need to continually ensure that the foster parents are aware of the agency's policies related to youth who identify as transgender and the requirements of appropriate and nonjudgmental service provision to these young people.

■ *Macro issues*: The social worker must attend to issues of policy practice. They would need to ensure that the foster agency (as well as a larger frame of all involved agencies) has explicit policies related to services for youth who identify as transgender. This can involve a number of steps, including the following:

- Evaluate current policies (or lack thereof) associated with working with youth who identify as transgender.
- Related, the social worker could help to develop quality assurance and compliance standards to make sure that policies are being implemented correctly.
- Examine best practices as laid out in social work literature (e.g., Fostering Transitions: A CWLA/Lambda Legal Joint Initiative, 2012; Mallon, 2009, 2010; Perron, 2015).
- Adopt policies that incorporate best practices and ensure all agency staff and foster parents are educated on the policies.

REFERENCES AND RESOURCES

Brill, S., & Kenney, L. (2016). *The transgender teen: A handbook for parents and professionals supporting transgender and non-binary teens.* Jersey City, NJ: Cleis Press.

Brill, S., & Pepper, R. (2008). *The transgender child: A handbook for families and professionals.* San Francisco, CA: Cleis Press.

Burdge, B. J. (2007). Bending gender, ending gender: Theoretical foundations for social work practice with the transgender community. *Social Work, 52*(3), 243–250.

Child Welfare League of America. (2012). *Recommended practices to promote the safety and well-being of lesbian, gay, bisexual, transgender and questioning (LGBTQ) youth and youth at risk of or living with HIV in child welfare settings.* Washington, DC: Author.

Cohen, J. A., Mannarino, A. P., & Deblinger, E. (2017). *Treating trauma and traumatic grief in children and adolescents* (2nd ed.). New York, NY: Guilford Press.

Diamond, L. M., Pardo, S. T., & Butterworth, M. R. (2011). Transgender experience and identity. In S. J. Schwartz, K. Luyckx, & V. L. Vignoles (Eds.), *Handbook of identity theory and research: Vol. 1. Structure and processes* (pp. 629–647). New York, NY: Springer.

Erickson-Schroth, L. (2014). *Trans bodies, trans selves: A resources for the transgender community.* New York, NY: Oxford University Press.

Fostering Transitions: A CWLA/Lambda Legal Joint Initiative. (2012). *Getting down to basics: Tools to support LGBTQ youth in care.* New York, NY: Lambda Legal & Child Welfare League of America.

Gretak, E. A., Kosciw, J. G., & Diaz, E. M. (2009). *Harsh realities: The experiences of transgender youth in our nation's schools.* New York, NY: GLSEN.

Hidalgo, M. A., Ehrensaft, D., Tishelman, A. C., Clark, L. F., Garofalo, R., Rosenthal, S. M., . . . Olson, J. (2013). The gender affirmative model: What we know and what we aim to learn. *Human Development, 56*(5), 285–290.

Mallon, G. P. (Ed.). (2009). *Social work practice with transgender and gender variant youth* (2nd ed.). New York, NY: Routledge.

Mallon, G. P. (2010). *LGBTQ youth issues: Practical guide for youth workers serving lesbian, gay, bisexual, transgender and questioning youth.* New York, NY: Child Welfare League of America.

National Association of Social Workers (NASW). (2015). Transgender and gender identity issues. In *Social work speaks* (10th ed.), pp. 303–310. Washington, DC: NASW Press.

Perron, S. (2015). *beFIERCE! A toolkit for providers working with LGBTQ foster youth.* San Francisco, CA: Walter S. Johnson Foundation.

Singh, A. A. (2012). Transgender youth of color and resilience: Negotiating oppression and finding support. *Sex Roles, 68*(11–12), 690–702.

Singh, A. A., & McKleroy, V. S. (2011). "Just getting out of bed is a revolutionary act": The resilience of transgender people of color who have survived traumatic life events. *Traumatology, 17*(2), 34–44.

Sullivan, C. A., Sommer, S., & Moff, J. (2001). *Youth in the margins: A report on the unmet needs of lesbian, gay, bisexual and transgender adolescents in foster care.* Washington, DC: Lambda Legal Defense & Education Fund.

Testa, R. J., Coolhart, D., & Peta, J. (2015). *The gender quest workbook: A guide for teens and young adults exploring gender identity.* Oakland, CA: Instant Help Books.

Travers, R., Guta, A., Flicker, S., Larkin, J., Lo, C., McCardell, S., & van der Meulen, E. (2010). Service provider views on issues and needs for lesbian, gay, bisexual, and transgender youth. *Canadian Journal of Human Sexuality, 19*(4), 191–198.

Woronoff, R., Estrada, R., & Sommer, S. (2006). *OUT of the margins: A report on the regional listening forums highlighting the experiences of lesbian, gay, bisexual, transgender and questioning youth in care.* Washington, DC: Child Welfare League of America.

8

LOVE AND LOSS(ES)

LAKE DZIENGEL

Walter is a sixty-eight-year-old Native American man who identifies as gay and is cisgender in appearance. He does not identify as Two-Spirit. Walter was raised both on and off his home reservation, and he entered the military after completing high school. He returned to live there a few years after serving in Vietnam, as the majority of his immediate family still remained on or near the reservation. Currently, Walter lives in a small midwestern city with his spouse, Joe, who is twenty years younger and identifies as Caucasian. They met through a mutual acquaintance, and Joe identified that he pursued the relationship with Walter despite the age difference. At the time they met, Walter lived in a rural area and a two-hour drive from where Joe resided, so Joe decided to move in with Walter. Walter and Joe have now been a couple for twenty-six years and own a home together. Walter retired after years of working in the service industry for the tribal community and, in part, due to becoming eligible for medical disability benefits. Joe is employed at a local hospital as a registered nurse. They are financially stable and do not need any additional professional health or social services at this time.

Walter and Joe initially lived and worked for the first twelve years of the relationship on the reservation, where Walter is an enrolled tribal member. Walter described that he was not "out" at work but that it was "common knowledge" that Joe and he were a couple. Joe attempted to integrate himself as a valued community member through volunteering and eventually became employed on the reservation. Despite this, they both admitted that being an interracial couple was more of a stressor than being in a same-sex relationship. Walter described that "outsiders" employed on the reservation were not welcomed and that white people were not easily accepted into the community. The tribe provided education funding for college education so they both began working on college degrees via a private, nonprofit college through distance education. Walter eventually completed a degree in business, while Joe pursued a degree in nursing. They also received other benefits provided to married couples, despite the fact that same-sex marriage had not yet been ratified.

Walter noted an ongoing stressor of reservation life was that they had few gay friends to associate with and sometimes were referred to as "the queens" by local people. In addition, Walter stated that his family took a while to "warm up" to Joe, as Joe was Walter's first long-term relationship and because Joe was white. While they interacted with Walter's family, Joe did not necessarily feel he was welcomed and was excluded from some events. Joe's family was somewhat more supportive and welcoming of Walter, despite their age, racial differences, and initially living more than two hours apart. Eventually, Walter and Joe moved back to the smaller city where they met, after Walter was released from employment with the reservation. Joe gained employment at a local hospital as an RN. This city was also where they had a larger social network of gay and lesbian friends, which continues to be a support system. While both cited examples of their families not being initially welcoming, they stated that over time, this changed to being more supportive. However, Joe's family seems more engaged and supportive of their relationship. They are legally married and report being monogamous.

Walter was certified as 80 percent disabled two years ago due to his military service in Vietnam and exposure to Agent Orange. He has had numerous health problems, including heart complications directly attributed to Agent Orange exposure and kidney cancer, which was diagnosed initially ten years after they became involved. The cancer cleared but recurred six years ago as metastatic renal cancer. Walter is medication- and treatment-compliant and receives services primarily from community-based medical providers and occasionally from the Veterans Administration Health Services (VA). Currently, he describes himself as in remission with regular scans to monitor any resurgence of cancer, although he stated, "I'm still fighting it." He cited that some of the biggest health care challenges were making sure Joe was included and respected as Walter's partner, despite Joe being Walter's durable power of attorney for health care. Joe cited several situations where he was restricted from access to Walter or needed to advocate on Walter's behalf. They legally married in 2013, and so being included in Walter's care became less of a problem; however, Joe consistently assesses whether they are being treated respectfully as a same-sex couple when they attend clinic appointments or are in hospitals. Walter does believe that his cancer recurrence was not identified as early as it could have been due to lack of follow-up by his health care provider and was unsure as to why this happened. Walter is currently covered by Joe's health insurance plan as well as VA benefits.

Both Walter and Joe realize they are very different in terms of their spirituality. Walter is proud of his Native American identity, and he is Christian and participates actively in a local faith community. Joe stated he is not religious but respects Walter's beliefs. They also have distinct communication styles: Walter is more reflective, is quieter, and has referred to himself as a "storyteller," whereas Joe described himself as very outgoing and more "moody." Walter credits his faith and his Native American heritage with his continuously being able to defy the odds of his diagnosis. He was prescribed (Western) medications that resulted in various negative side effects; at one point, he was confined to a wheelchair due to the cancer affecting his spine. He is currently ambulatory and optimistic about his future health needs, although he acknowledges that his condition will eventually result in death. In kind, Walter described that Joe and he have always lived their life "in increments," that is, they make five-year goals and plans. This has become more important given Walter's ongoing problems with cancer. He said they are very compatible in managing money and financial planning, and they have identified several action steps to ensure that Joe has financial stability after Walter's death. At this point, Walter remains optimistic and realistic. Joe stated he realized long ago that getting involved with an older man would have challenges but that he was not prepared for the cancer: he hates it and how it has taken so much away from Walter, and he has some fears associated with Walter's health, as well as the future. Joe indicated that sometimes he does not want to go out and do things with other people because he wants to be home with Walter, who is not able to be as physically active and becomes fatigued more easily. He worries about what would happen if he were not around and Walter had a heart attack. Joe stated he occasionally wonders how much time they have left and noted that Walter used to be more muscular and physically fit. Thus, Joe has watched cancer change Walter's appearance. Joe was also very clear that Walter is his love, and he cannot imagine ever being so close to someone again. Joe cited using his head and clinical thinking as a protective feature at times to avoid the emotional pain and fear about Walter's health. Neither of them expressed a desire or need to be involved in supportive counseling at this time.

REFLEXIVE NOTE

The author met Walter and Joe as part of a research project they were completing on same-sex couple resiliency and losses. The couple shared their experiences, both individually and then as a couple, through an extensive interview. Having been a medical social worker in chronic health and end-of-life care, the author was able to extrapolate and identify potential future concerns. Focused discussion on this case can be considered through the role of either a medical or hospice social worker.

GUIDING QUESTIONS

- Thinking through a lens of social construction, what might be some potential barriers that hindered supports for Joe and Walter as an interracial couple? As a same-sex couple?
- Walter is a veteran and Native American as well as gay. How do these aspects intersect in his relationships with his family, his health care, or with his spirituality? What else would you want to know about these identities?
- What ethical obligations must health care providers consider in providing respectful care and inclusion of partners for same-sex couples, whether or not they are legally married?

- What are some potential losses that Walter and Joe have already experienced individually and as a couple? How might anticipatory grief affect how they interact with each other as couple?
- Ambiguous losses are not easily identified and not necessarily related to a death. Ambiguity in relationships and supports can be a factor that leads to an ambiguous loss. What might be some sources or contributing elements of ambiguity for Walter and Joe? Do you think they have experienced any ambiguous losses?

CASE FORMULATION

Generalist Formulation

Both Walter and Joe have established strong individual identities, as well as an enduring couple identity that resulted in Walter becoming more out to his family as a gay man over time. Neither identified any personal trauma or negative coping strategies, but both recognized the discrimination they experienced as an interracial couple and as a same-sex couple. While both of their families were not supportive initially, Walter's family was less so. Joe believed they tried to interfere, at times, in the relationship in hopes that Joe would leave. Moving off the reservation provided more social supports, especially given Walter's cancer diagnosis, as well as a stable income and health insurance for both Joe and Walter.

From the beginning of their relationship, Walter and Joe appeared very compatible in their personal goals and found joy in their relationship despite early stressors. They faced challenges of racism, homophobia, and even ageism, given the difference in their ages. Joe described their personality differences, with Walter being like "the salt of the earth and grounded . . . I [Joe] am like the wind . . . but we both value our relationship. We have always put our relationship first." An unexpected problem was Walter's health crisis ten years into their relationship that seemed to resolve but then reemerged six years ago. When Walter was hospitalized due to heart complications, they were told he might live another year. Thus, they have needed to address multiple factors for the past six years, including financial, estate, and burial planning. They have been very pragmatic and dealt with homophobia in their employment and in health care settings regarding Walter's care. Joe has established himself as a medical advocate and partner for Walter, but he realizes this is stressful. Joe's status as an RN has given him skills in being able to identify and advocate for Walter's needs. He also has a personality that is not afraid to advocate on behalf of their couple status and Walter's treatment. He described that he somewhat had to "learn" how to do this but now is very comfortable in that role. What Joe also seems to realize is that sometimes he can "get into [my] nurse head and talk very clinically." Joe recognized that this is a protective factor and stated he has not let himself experience some of the emotional impact. Walter's beliefs seem to buoy him through difficult times, and he sees this as a source of strength. Joe seems to rely more on his intellect and his love for Walter and stated he will "be lost" without him.

Culturally Responsive and Queer-Affirmative Formulation

Walter's Native American identity is connected largely to his emotional and cultural ties to his family and somewhat to his spirituality. He seems to have blended indigenous beliefs with a strong Christian identity (Lutheran), and he participates in a structured community. He was raised Catholic, but he found that religious system too oppressive for people who identify as LGBTQ+. Walter describes spirituality as a belief system rather than a faith. He also described himself as a storyteller, as part of his cultural identity as Native American. Joe is Caucasian, and the interracial aspect of their relationship has caused them some stress, with Joe stating that after Walter dies, he likely will not interact with Walter's family anymore. This uneasiness could result in discord between Walter's family and Joe as Walter's health deteriorates. Walter is close to his family, but their relationship remains somewhat strained and could become a significant stressor.

As a same-sex and interracial couple, Walter and Joe have faced and continue to face a very difficult diagnosis. Their age difference has occasionally resulted in them being perceived as father and son or as brothers. As a gay couple, Joe has consistently advocated in decisions regarding Walter's care due to disenfranchisement of their relationship (see Almack, Seymour, & Bellamy, 2010); for example, once, before they were married and on vacation in another state, Joe experienced being barred from seeing Walter in the hospital because he was not considered a relative. Now that they are married, this is not a legal concern. Still, Joe is keenly aware of the treatment and level of (dis)respect demonstrated by care providers. As a result, they constantly monitor for any homophobia and disparate treatment. They appear to have a good network of friends, and Joe's family has been more demonstrative in providing emotional support over the years. Both are vocal about their gay identities, yet they acknowledged that while Walter is entitled to VA care, they do not often use VA services due to the military overtones. Joe, in particular, noted the VA was "dysfunctional" and that they had received care from a provider who did not include Joe in discussions. Joe perceived this as homophobia. Walter stated that the VA put him on medications that resulted in severe side effects, and so he did not trust their treatment protocols. In addition, VA services are not easily accessible due to physical distance.

Neither Joe nor Walter actively seek support from family or friends in regard to Walter's health needs. They appear to be managing this mostly on their own. Some of Walter's care and hospitalizations have also taken place in locations three hours or more from their home residence and thus likely inhibited much family visiting or engagement. As Walter's health declines, they may seek to be more engaged, which could result in some emotional support from a social worker to address any potential conflicts. While they have been together for twenty-six years and married recently, Walter's mother is Catholic and still does not seem very comfortable with their relationship. This is difficult for Walter as he cares for her deeply. A hospice social worker would be valuable in end-of-life care for both Walter and Joe in managing family interactions. Given Joe has often been a primary caregiver and advocate, he would likely benefit from emotional supports as Walter approaches end of life.

TREATMENT AND ACTION PLANNING

- *Resilience*: Walter and Joe's strength and resilience to manage ongoing health concerns and occasional crisis are reflective of the longevity, complementary nature of their communication styles, and compatibility in their relationship (Dziengel, 2012). Walter displays life skills in managing stressors, which is not unusual for older gay or lesbian identified adults who gain competence and adaptability despite discrimination based on sexuality (Metlife Mature Market Institute, 2010) and as a Native American man who has also faced racism throughout his life (see Frost, Lehavot, & Meyer, 2015). Moreover, Joe demonstrates resilience and compatibility with Walter, and they have built an emotionally and physically supportive environment over time. This level of resilience and personal standpoint that they can manage stressors should be considered a resource. Still, social work services for this couple might be indicated in the future as Walter's health deteriorates.

- *Life span perspective*: In providing (future) social work services, it would be helpful to have a concrete conversation about possible case management needs responsive to their couplehood as a whole but also responsive to their individual places on the life span continuum. Recognizing the strengths within a same-sex couple relationship, particularly related to their level of trust within the relationship, and their ego strength must be reinforced as a resource (Hash & Rogers, 2013), as well as examining their strengths and resources built as a couple over time (Dziengel, 2012). Despite the difference in ages, Walter and Joe have also consistently supported each other over time through a variety of difficult situations and appear to have adapted to aging together. One stated concern was how Joe would manage after Walter's death. Walter is mostly concerned about Joe's monetary stability, while Joe is wondering about his future emotional health without a partner at middle age. It would be helpful to initiate or hold space for these topics in dialogue to see if possible supportive services or resources (e.g., in-home assistance/respite care, support group) would be welcomed by both or either of them.

- *Affirming intersectional practice*: It would be important to cultivate validation for, attention to, and space for the intersections that exist within and around Walter in terms of culture, sexuality, stressors, and his own be/coming. Critical to Walter's care is acknowledging his Native American identity and the intersections of racism, heterosexism, and his military service. While he lived and worked on the reservation before meeting Joe, he was not out, and this was a personal stressor, particularly with his family. Walter had also carefully navigated military service as a young man and had remained fairly closeted until he met Joe in his late forties. Walter was unsure if some of his substandard medical care experiences related to his racial identity or because he was in a same-sex relationship. In fact, it is even more possible that both may have contributed to negative interactions with health providers.

In addition, Joe and Walter have supported each other for twenty-six years, and a part of their individual and couple development has been a be/coming-out process (Dziengel, 2015). Disclosing sexual orientation seems to reduce the risk of mental health factors in chronic health conditions (Hoy-Ellis & Fredriksen-Goldsen, 2016). Ongoing fear of discrimination or disrespect could limit how Joe and Walter access needed services, especially as Walter's health declines. Walter has relied on his faith community and is part of a group of LGBT elders. These are strong networks that should be encouraged and supported as he gains both affirmation and spiritual strength from these resources.

In kind, a social worker must act as a strong advocate for respectful, equitable, and just treatment in hospital and clinical care settings. Using VA services, to which Walter is entitled, could ease their financial burden. While these services are somewhat limited in physical access, Joe was more outspoken about his perceptions that these services had too much of a negative overtone toward gay patients and couples. In addition, as Walter's health deteriorates, there may come a time when his family seeks more interaction or wants to be part of his care team. This will require consideration of Native American standpoints and, potentially, a religious perspective. A social worker will need to be attentive to the multiple intersecting identities and assisting both Walter and Joe in navigating health care needs, family involvement, and affirming both their couple and individual identities. Should Walter and Joe seek hospice care at some point, a social worker will need to affirm and support their relationship and viewpoints and may need to collaborate with spiritual providers.

■ *Grief, loss, and ambiguity*: Parallel to any case management, brokering, or advocacy services, there is an indication here for potential (brief) talk therapy services. Given Walter's self-described nature as a "storyteller" and through interactions with both of them, narrative theory and methods would be very appropriate, in conjunction with some grief counseling. Narrative theory allows for full exploration from the personal standpoint, affirms experiences, helps to make meaning of events, and is culturally responsive (Frost, 2011). A factor for both Walter and Joe is anticipatory grief (Worden, 2009), compounded by having to manage ambiguity in relationships with family members over time (Boss, 2006). Both Joe and Walter acknowledged that being an interracial and same-sex couple strained some family and friendship relationships. This level of ambiguity of support can be difficult to identify, navigate, and manage, particularly for same-sex couples (Boss, 2006; Dziengel, 2012). As an additional stressor, if people are not able to adapt or reconcile these ambiguities, this can lead to ambiguous losses: those losses that are not easily identified, are unresolved, and create ongoing discomfort, complexity, and distress.

Ambiguous losses can result in problems such as loss of meaning, decreased sense of control, ongoing ambivalence, reduced attachments, confusion about roles and identity, and a loss of hope (Boss, 2006). Addressing these requires clear communication and acknowledgment of the loss(es). People often think of loss as death rather than a loss of relationship. Ambiguous loss methods focus on examining events and relationships that may be laden with ambiguity and a lack of clarity, and they help to "normalize" the ambiguity (Boss, 2006). Individuals explore if they are experiencing communication conflicts or duality in feelings and experiences (e.g., I love my family and they make me so mad). This enables the person to work on strategies to cope with unresolved emotions and problematic communication or to build resilience despite ambiguity of support from others. For same-sex couples, this could be exhibited by family members making general statements of affection and caring but with conditions like "don't be too out," "don't talk about your relationship," or excluding a partner from a family photo. To that end, a social worker could talk with both Walter and Joe about relationships, emotions, or personal factors that may seem unresolved for them over time to offset conflicts with family or friends, as Walter's health declines. This would also decrease any sense of self-blame and help them to identify the psychological supports that are available during this time. Walter and Joe do spend time with family, but neither of them identified family or friends as a significant source of emotional or physical support specific to Walter's health care over the years.

Walter and Joe identify ambiguity in relationships with family and friends but do not identify ambiguous losses. However, they are currently focused on the status of Walter's health and how that affects them day to day. However, it is a reality that some same-sex couples face difficulties at end-of-life care, particularly with homophobia, exclusion, and lack of relationship support (Bristowe, Marshall, & Harding, 2016). A possible topic to explore may be how Walter feels about leaving his original faith system and its treatment of gay people. His family still practices that faith and could present a future conflict in end-of-life care should his family seek to be actively involved in his care. Also, he identifies with his Native American ancestry, and this may be an additional loss that could emerge as an unresolved conflict. Walter left reservation life to move with Joe but also because he felt somewhat isolated as a gay man and had been very closeted, whereas now he is much more open and confident in his identity. These may simply be ongoing areas of ambiguity. It would be helpful for a social worker to explore these concepts and potentially help both Walter and Joe with several core components found in ambiguous loss theory (Boss, 2006). These components include normalizing any negative feelings, with a continued focus on their couple and individual resiliency. Furthermore, this approach could help them find meaning in their experience, acknowledge the changes of their identities over time, recognize any ongoing ambivalence, and reinforce coping strategies. Finally, finding hope and forgiveness are all elements that could be useful for both Walter and Joe to offset any possibility that unresolved family or friendship conflicts might lead to an ambiguous loss in the future.

RESOURCES

Indigenous Ways of Knowing. (2017). Tribal equity toolkit 3.0: Tribal resolutions and codes to support Two-Spirit and LGBTQ justice in Indian Country. Retrieved from http://www.thetaskforce.org/wp-content/uploads/2014/09/TET3.0.pdf

Red Circle Project (HIV Resource): http://redcircleproject.org

REFERENCES

Almack, K., Seymour, J., & Bellamy, G. (2010). Exploring the impact of sexual orientation on experiences and concerns about end of life care and on bereavement for lesbian, gay and bisexual older people. *Sociology, 44*(5), 908–924.

Boss, P. (2006). *Loss, trauma and resilience: Therapeutic work with ambiguous loss.* New York, NY: Norton.

Bristowe, K., Marshall, S., & Harding, R. (2016). The bereavement experiences of lesbian, gay, bisexual and/or trans* people who have lost a partner: A systematic review, thematic synthesis and modeling of the literature. *Palliative Medicine, 30*(8), 730–744.

Dziengel, L. (2012). Resilience, ambiguous loss and older same-sex couples: The resilience constellation model. *Journal of Social Service Research, 38*(1), 74–88.

Dziengel, L. (2015). A be/coming out model: Assessing factors of resilience and ambiguity. *Journal of Gay and Lesbian Social Services, 27*(3), 302–325.

Dziengel, L. (2016, February 9). *Ambiguous loss and resiliency in LGBTQ aging.* Retrieved from http://asaging.org/blog/ambiguous-loss-and-resiliency-lgbtq-aging

Frost, D. M. (2011). Stigma and intimacy in same-sex relationships: A narrative approach. *Journal of Family Psychology, 25*(1), 1–19.

Frost, D. M., Lehavot, K., & Meyer, I. H. (2015). Minority stress and physical health among sexual minority individuals. *Journal of Behavioral Medicine, 38,* 1–8.

Hash, K. M., & Rogers, A. (2013). Clinical practice with older LGBT clients: Overcoming lifelong stigma through strength and resilience. *Clinical Social Work Journal, 41,* 249–257.

Hoy-Ellis, C. P., & Fredriksen-Goldsen, K. I. (2016). Lesbian, gay and bisexual older adults: Linking internal minority stressors, chronic health conditions and stress. *Aging and Mental Health, 20*(11), 1119–1130.

Metlife Mature Market Institute. (2010). *Still out, still aging: The Metlife study of lesbian, gay, bisexual, and transgendered baby boomers.* Westport, CT: Metlife.

Worden, J. W. (2009). *Grief counseling and grief therapy: A handbook for the mental health practitioner* (4th ed.). New York, NY: Springer.

9

FAMILY DINNERS

SHANNA K. KATTARI

T wo parents are concerned about their son Jayden, who is fifteen years old. Jayden is Latino, was assigned a male gender identity at birth, and is currently attending the neighborhood public high school in their midsized Southwest city. He is a solid B student and participates in the theater program at his high school. His parents, Cristina and Daniel, are a heterosexual Latino couple who have been married for eighteen years; Jayden is their only child. They are second-generation U.S. citizens, both from parents who emigrated from Mexico; they speak both English and Spanish in their home. The family is middle class, with both parents working full-time. The parents have shared that it is important to them to have strong family connections; therefore, they make sure to have dinner together every night, for example. Cristina and Daniel attend a Catholic church in their community every Sunday but do not particularly identify as strongly religious. Jayden attended Confraternity of Christian Doctrine (religious education classes) and Sunday school for several years but now tells his parents he is "no longer interested in attending church."

Cristina and Daniel tell you that, starting about a year ago, Jayden began to wear eyeliner to school, occasionally would wear dresses, spent a lot of time in the school's theater club, and would hang out almost exclusively with young women, both inside and outside of school. Originally thinking it was "just a phase," they have become very concerned that Jayden might be bullied at school because of his (gender) presentation, although they have no proof of any specific issues occurring. Both parents believe that Jayden may be gay or may be like "those transgender people" they have seen on TV. They are clear that they love and support their son, but they want someone to "help" him and "fix" him so that he will fit in at school. While Jayden is outgoing and engaged at school, he is not interested in speaking to his parents about his sexual orientation or gender identity; he has started to avoid family dinners because of his frustration with his parents' questions about why he dresses the way he does and hangs out with the people with whom he chooses to spend time. Instead, he spends a lot of time on the Internet, including using social media and blogging. He shares that, because his grades are fine and he is happy with his friend group, it is none of his parents' business what he wears or how he identifies.

GUIDING QUESTIONS

- What other information would be helpful in your assessment and for your consideration?
- Depending on who is your client, would you meet with them all together or individually?
- How might culture (i.e., Mexican, Latino, Catholic) be used as a lens to conceptualize both what the parents as well as Jayden himself are experiencing, individually and collectively?

  - How is gender understood in their Mexican local, regional, and national cultures?

- Which models or approaches might be helpful here to un-pack this clinical situation as well as shed light on processing the struggles this family is facing? What about Jayden specifically?
- How may religion be a source of both strength and harm in this case? How might it contribute to or derail resiliency? What considerations do you find depending on how LGBTQ+ affirmative or oppressive their religion, denomination, and local church are?
- Who else might you want to reach out to or involve in your conversations or connecting to resources?
- What would you do if Cristina and Daniel wanted to pursue conversion/reparative therapy? Note: Both the National Association of Social Workers (NASW) and Council on Social Work Education have taken positions against this type of "therapy," which has proven to be harmful (NASW, 2015).

CASE FORMULATION

Generalist Formulation

Jayden is either gay, transgender, or a combination therein. He has not yet been able, or does not feel comfortable enough, to come out to his parents. The fact that his parents are Latino and strongly religious may equally be a protective factor in terms of familial connection as well as a risk factor in terms of increasing stigma and nonacceptance, thus increasing stress for Jayden. The focus of clinical attention here should be on facilitating Jayden coming out to his parents, who will need to learn to accept him if they want him to continue to be part of their family.

Culturally Responsive and Queer-Affirmative Formulation

Gender identity and gender presentation are more of a spectrum and exist outside of a binary. Jayden is exploring a variety of gender expressions and/or identities, and he seems to be happy and authentic. His grades have not slipped. Also, even if there are negative reactions from his peers, he appears to be incredibly resilient and has made a strong group of friends in theater who support him. He may or may not be LGBTQ+, but he does not yet seem ready to come out to his family if he is. This may be motivated by some expected fear about how they could react, or he may still be exploring his identities and not know how to answer his family's questions. Understandably, he may have hesitation due to being a teenager. Still, the fact that Jayden's parents are involved in his life and notice him pulling away from family time suggests that they genuinely care about him and want what is best for him. While there may be a clash in how Jayden "versus" his parents view support, both parties have strong connections, which bodes well for therapy. The focus here would be equally (if not more) on the parents, the family unit, as well as Jayden.

TREATMENT AND ACTION PLANNING

- *Identify "the client"*: It is imperative to discern who is, in fact, the client; it may be Jayden, Jayden's parents, or the family system. If Jayden is the client, it would be necessary to discern to what extent the parents are involved in the care plan as well as any given session. This would begin with a conversation about confidentiality laws (in the social worker's state of practice) and minors who engage with mental health care. If the parents are the client, it would be helpful to identify any referral for individual therapy for Jayden, as indicated. Likewise, if Jayden is the client, a referral to family therapy may be warranted. If Jayden is not your client, define what legal and ethical obligations you have to him and what steps you might take to meet these obligations.

- Likewise, it is imperative to initially engage all of them in a discussion about using authentic pronouns and then to model their use and actively practice in session how to use them. For example, see https://uwm.edu/lgbtrc/support/gender-pronouns/.

- Similarly, offer discussion on the differences and nuances among gender identity, gender expressions, sexual orientation, and romantic orientation (among other identities along these continua). A helpful resource could be the Gender Unicorn, http://www.transstudent.org/gender.

■ *Assessment*: Regardless of how the client/system is approached and defined, an affirmative assessment needs to include the following considerations and conversations:

- Assess the parents: It is imperative to gain an accurate sense of how the parents feel about Jayden on the whole and, more specifically, Jayden should she/he/they come out as gay/bi/queer, as transgender, and/or as gender nonconforming. It would be helpful to understand in what ways their non/acceptance could be a barrier and (mental health) risk factor for Jayden. A young person's ability to accept their self depends on the belief that they will ultimately be accepted and loved despite those differences (Malyon, 1981). See the work on minority stress (Alessi, 2014).

- Assess everyone's "coming out": Related to this, it is necessary to assess the state of "coming out" that the parents may be in themselves. It is not uncommon that parents and other allied family or fictive kin members may have their own process to engage with in terms of coming to accept their loved one who may be LGBTQGNC as well as becoming their own allied self.

  o Arlene Istar Lev (2004) proposes a six-stage model for the process of transgender identification, including milestones and coming out. This model applies to transgender individuals, their families, and clinicians.

  o Part of considering the status of the parents would also be about figuring out what sorts of (negative) effects this situation has had on the couple system (i.e., the marriage). Depending on the salience and intensity, this may warrant a referral to couples and/or family therapy, sooner rather than later.

  o For Jayden specifically, it is important to offer space to process, as needed, any coming out or coming into certain identities. The act of coming out enables individuals to live more truthfully and openly, leads to greater happiness, and ameliorates many potential physical and mental/ emotional health concerns (Cox, Dewaele, van Houtte, & Vincke, 2011; D'Augelli & Grossman, 2001; Herek, 1988; Meyer, 2003; Proctor & Groze, 1994; Remafedi, 1987). For LGBTQ+ youth, the dread of rejection of core aspects of their identity (e.g., sexuality, gender) can result in a variety of desperate coping or hiding strategies (Martin, 1982). Thus, it is necessary to explicitly discuss with parents the importance of their acceptance and support for Jayden's overall mental health and success (Ryan, Huebner, Diaz, & Sanchez, 2009).

- Quite critically, some practitioners may have to support clients through periods of actually "not coming out" for their own safety (e.g., a youth who may be struggling with coming out to hostile parents and risks being kicked out of their home).
- Besides identifying where potential risks may be, this process also involves identifying and mobilizing available networks of family or friends who may be supportive or allies when it is time to come out.

• Assess social and other supports: While extending support and acceptance, it is important to gain a thorough understanding about the social and other trusted supports that everyone has, that is, Jayden and each parent.

  o As for Jayden, what about school? Peers? Friendships? Can his friends be of support to him? How do others treat him?

    For most young LGBTQ+ individuals today, the first disclosures of suspected sexual orientation or gender variance take place in conversations with "trusted friends" online (Craig & McInroy, 2014; Egan, 2000; Hillier & Harrison, 2007).

  o As for the parents, do they have their own social supports? More formalized supports like groups at their church? Trusted family members?

  o It may be helpful to broker information and provide advocacy for support groups locally for parents, Jayden, and family. A local or regional LGBTQ+ center may be a good place to start for educational resources, parent groups, groups for Jayden, a drop-in program, or other basic emotional support and advice. Jayden's school may also be a source of support; it may have queer-straight alliances and gay-straight alliances. For example, see:

- GSA Network, http://gsanetwork.org/resources/build
  ing-your-gsa/what-gsa
- Parents and Friends of Lesbians and Gays, https://
  www.pflag.org/
- Depending how religious the parents are, they may
  find support through a Catholic (or other denomination) organization such as Dignity USA, www.dignity
  usa.org.

■ *Safety, risk*: It is imperative to have a strong understanding of
historical and/or contemporary issues of safety for Jayden. This
begins with biopsychosocial assessment and psychoeducation
with the entire family.

- Assess the presence, nature, and extent of bullying or other
  harassment that Jayden experiences. Does Jayden feel safe at
  school? At home? See Toomey, McGuire, and Russell (2012)
  and Toomey, Ryan, Diaz, Card, and Russell (2010).
- Assess the salience and nature of microaggressions at home,
  at school, and in the community. What type of language is
  being used by Jayden's peers, teachers, and so on? See Rockquemore (2016) and Sue (2010).
- Assess the signs and/or self-reports of emotional distress, coping skills, clinically diagnosable mood or anxiety disorders,
  and self-harming behaviors. Consider the higher risks for suicidality, depression, and self-harm for LGBTQ+ youth. Trevor
  Project, www.thetrevorproject.org/.
- Based on the biopsychosocial assessment, a conversation
  with both the parents as well as Jayden may be warranted, at
  some point, about sexuality, sexually transmitted infections,
  and safer sex practices. This conversation may be a joint
  session or something done individually with the parents in

terms of coaching and then possibly with Jayden. To this point, a conversation about sexuality, health, family planning, and prevention methods necessarily will be part of the considerations here. See the discussion on inclusive sexuality education for LGBTQ+ youth, for example, at http://www.hrc.org/resources/a-call-to-action-lgbtq-youth-need-inclusive-sex-education.

- *Approach*: In this moment, it would be helpful to gain a better sense of the goals of therapy and in particular the kinds of change that each family member may want to make or see as issues for therapy. To that end, motivational interviewing could assist in clarifying everyone's goals and what their needs may be to move forward (Naar-King & Suarez, 2011). Likewise, as issues or "problems" are identified and the intervention plan is crafted, it is helpful to engender an approach that is grounded in an intersectional, culturally responsive lens.

  - For many LGBTQ+ individuals, managing multiple identities based on sexuality, race/ethnicity, religion, and other intersecting factors may significantly increase the difficulty of typical tasks associated with identity development and coming-out processes.
  - Wallace, Carter, Nanín, Keller, and Alleyne (2002) found that among LGBTQ+ people of color, the primacy of sexual identities remained secondary to other identities and roles. This is to say, racial/ethnic identities are prioritized over sexuality in response to the many psychosocial and environmental barriers associated with race, ethnicity, and socioeconomic status.
  - Related to this, given the religiosity of Jayden's household, it is important to tend to the ways in which they may negotiate coming out as LGBTQ+ while also identifying as religiously

observant or dealing with parents who are. The virulent anti-gay and transphobic rhetoric of most religious doctrine is among the most damaging and condemning of all social messages an LGBTQ+ person encounters (Mahaffy, 1996). See Austin and Craig (2015); Craig, Austin, and Alessi (2013); Duarté-Vélez, Bernal, and Bonilla (2010); and Sue, Rasheed, and Rasheed (2015).

RESOURCES

Gender Spectrum: https://www.genderspectrum.org/
GLSEN. When a Student Comes Out to You: http://www.glsen.org/blog
/when-student-comes-out-youtoday-or-any-day
HealthyChildren: https://www.healthychildren.org/English/ages-stages
/gradeschool/Pages/Gender-Non-Conforming-Transgender-Children
.aspx
HRC. Coming Out Issues for Latinos and Latinas: www.hrc.org/resources
/family-and-coming-out-issues-for-latinas-and-latinos
Human Rights Campaign. A Resource Guide to Coming Out: http://www
.hrc.org/resources/resource-guide-to-coming-out
Lambda Legal. Supporting trans/GNC youth: http://www.lambdalegal.org
/know-your-rights/article/youth-tgnc
LULAC. LGBT: http://lulac.org/programs/lgbt/
Somos Familia: http://www.somosfamiliabay.org/wordpress/?page_id=7
Trans Youth Equality Foundation: www.transyouthequality.org
Trans Youth Family Allies: www.imatyfa.org/

REFERENCES

Alessi, E. J. (2014). A framework for incorporating minority stress theory into treatment with sexual minority clients. *Journal of Gay & Lesbian Mental Health, 18*, 47–66.

Austin, A., & Craig, S. L. (2015). Empirically supported interventions for sexual and gender minority youth. *Journal of Evidence-Informed Social Work, 12*(6), 567–578.

Cox, N., Dewaele, A, van Houtte, M., & Vincke, J. (2011). Stress-related growth, coming out, and internalized homonegativity in lesbian, gay, and bisexual youth: An examination of stress-related growth within the minority stress model. *Journal of Homosexuality, 58*(1), 117–137.

Craig, S. L., Austin, A., & Alessi, E. (2013). Gay affirmative cognitive behavioral therapy for sexual minority youth: A clinical adaptation. *Clinical Social Work Journal, 41*(3), 258–266.

Craig, S. L., & McInroy, L. (2014). You can form a part of yourself online: The influence of new media on identity development and coming out for LGBT youth. *Journal of Gay & Lesbian Mental Health, 18*, 95–109.

D'Augelli, A. R., & Grossman, A. H. (2001). Disclosure of sexual orientation, victimization, and mental health among lesbian, gay, and bisexual older adults. *Journal of Interpersonal Violence, 16*, 1008–1027.

Duarté-Vélez, Y., Bernal, G., & Bonilla, K. (2010). Culturally adapted cognitive-behavior therapy: Integrating sexual, spiritual, and family identities in an evidence-based treatment of a depressed Latino adolescent. *Journal of Clinical Psychology, 66*(8), 895–906.

Egan, J. (2000, December 10). Lonely gay teen seeking same: How Jeffrey found friendship, sex, heartache—and himself—online. *New York Times Magazine*, pp. 110–118.

Herek, G. M. (1988). Stigma, prejudice, and violence against lesbians and gay men. In J. C. Gonsiorek & J. D. Weinrick (Eds.), *Homosexuality: Research implications for public policy* (pp. 60–80). Newbury Park, CA: Sage.

Hillier, L., & Harrison, L. (2007). Building realities less limited than their own: Young people practicing same-sex attraction on the Internet. *Sexualities, 10*(1), 82–100.

Jackson, D., & Sullivan, R. (1994). Developmental implications of homophobia for lesbian and gay adolescents: Issues in policy and practice. *Journal of Gay and Lesbian Social Services, 1*(3–4), 93–109.

Lev, A. I. (2004). *Transgender emergence: Therapeutic guidelines for working with gender-variant people and their families*. Binghamton, NY: Haworth Press.

Mahaffy, K. A. (1996). Cognitive dissonance and its resolution: A study of lesbian Christians. *Journal for the Scientific Study of Religion, 35*(4), 392–402.

Malyon, A. K. (1981). The homosexual adolescent: Developmental issues and social bias. *Child Welfare, 60*(5), 321–330.

Martin, A. D. (1982). Learning to hide: The socialization of the gay adolescent. *Adolescent Psychiatry, 10*, 52–65.

Meyer, I. H. (2003). Prejudice, social stress, and mental health in lesbian, gay, and bisexual populations: Conceptual issues and research evidence. *Psychological Bulletin, 129*(5), 674–697.

Naar-King, S., & Suarez, M. (2011). *Motivational interviewing with adolescents and young adults.* New York, NY: Guilford Press.

Proctor, C. D., & Groze, V. K. (1994). Risk factors for suicide among gay, lesbian, and bisexual youths. *Social Work, 39*(5), 504–513.

Remafedi, G. (1987). Adolescent homosexuality: Psychosocial and medical implications. *Pediatrics, 79*(3), 331–337.

Rockquemore, K. A. (2016). How to be an ally to someone experiencing microaggressions. *Inside Higher Ed.* Retrieved from https://www.inside highered.com/advice/2016/04/13/how-be-ally-someone-experiencing -microaggressions-essay

Ryan, C., Huebner, D., Diaz, R. M., & Sanchez, J. (2009). Family rejection as a predictor of negative health outcomes in white and Latino lesbian, gay, and bisexual young adults. *Pediatrics, 123*(1), 346–352.

Sue, D. W. (2010). *Microaggressions in everyday life: Race, gender, and sexual orientation.* Hoboken, NJ: Wiley.

Sue, D. W., Rasheed, M. N., & Rasheed, J. M. (2015). *Multicultural social work practice: A competency-based approach to diversity and social justice.* Hoboken, NJ: Wiley.

Toomey, R. B., McGuire, J. K., & Russell, S. T. (2012). Heteronormativity, school climates, and perceived safety for gender nonconforming peers. *Journal of Adolescence, 35*(1), 187–196.

Toomey, R. B., Ryan, C., Diaz, R. M., Card, N. A., & Russell, S. T. (2010). Gender-nonconforming lesbian, gay, bisexual, and transgender youth: School victimization and young adult psychosocial adjustment. *Developmental Psychology, 46*(6), 1580.

Wallace, B., Carter, R., Nanín, J., Keller, R., & Alleyne, V. (2002). Identity development for "diverse and different others": Integrating stages of change, motivational interviewing, and identity theories for race, people of color, sexual orientation, and disability. In B. Wallace & R. Carter (Eds.), *Understanding and dealing with violence: A multicultural approach* (pp. 41–91). Thousand Oaks, CA: Sage Publications.

10

NEVER GOOD ENOUGH

HENRY W. KRONNER

Scott reports that he is a fifty-five-year-old, white, Jewish man who grew up in the Midwestern United States. He reports marrying Lucy when he was twenty years old and she was nineteen years old; they were married for eight years and they had two children (Susan, who is now thirty-three, and Albert, who is thirty). Scott said he is creative and that he has worked in design for his whole adult life, either as an interior designer for his own clients or using his skills in large retail companies. He reports that at age twenty-eight, he divorced his wife when he realized he could no longer remain in a heterosexual marriage due to him being gay. He reported that he had a few sexual encounters with men before their marriage and a few encounters during the marriage. He reported that Lucy was not accepting at first, but "she understands the reason I divorced her, and she accepts me." Both kids reportedly accept their father's decision to divorce and be an out, gay man.

Scott reports that his childhood was very dysfunctional; he reports having an emotionally distant father, who at times was emotionally and verbally abusive, but it was his mother who was the most "verbally and emotionally abusive." For example, when he saw the play *August: Osage County*, he was so distressed as it seemed to perfectly depict his mother. He said he did not understand how others were laughing, as he was seeing a real story unfold before him. Furthermore, he said that he learned that he "could never do anything right," "never be good enough," and that, in order not to be "attacked," "judged," or "shamed," he would keep out of her way or try to "read" her to decide how to proceed.

He is of average height (5′8″) and slightly overweight. He has dark brown hair that he appears to dye, and his clothes are of the best quality, style, and design as he reports he shops only at "high-end" department stores. His presents as well groomed and stylish, stating that being "put together" is very important to him. Due to his focus on his appearance, his weight seems to cause him distress and self-judgment. His need to present so well physically seems to be a coping strategy to hide all the hurt, guilt, and shame that he carries every day. Last, he reports being diagnosed with HIV five years ago, and this also seems to be another way he feels both guilt and shame for his actions and for himself. He reports he did not "go on medication" for several years as his T-cell counts were high; he started taking HIV medications two years ago and reports that he is very compliant with the medication regimen.

He reports having friends but that he is challenged to keep friends for extended periods of time. Over the many years of therapy, he reports numerous gay male friends who cease to be friends today. This seems to be due, in part, to his choice of friends and partly due to his constant judgment of them; they often do not seem to meet his apparent unrealistic requirements in terms of emotional support, intelligence, and maturity, among other qualities. He reports having some friends for many years (e.g., twenty to thirty-five years), and these are often cis-female friends; he judges them less often and they provide support, care, and a nonjudgmental attitude toward him.

He reports working a full-time job in sales and design. Even though he reports losing two major jobs (one in which he was fired and one in which he was laid off), he always finds a way to obtain a new job and earn money to pay his bills. He presents as very resourceful, hardworking, and dedicated.

In therapy, he comes to session sharing his challenges during the week, and he works to connect the challenges to his past and look at ways he can make changes. Scott often presents as resistant because he fears that he cannot make change in his life; he worries that if he makes change, his life still will not be different or improved. He often does not appear very cohesive and can be easily fragmented by any statement or action by another that he interprets to be hurtful or judgmental. Over the course of ten years, he has addressed his self-perception and related poor self-concept. Through therapy, he has been able to address his depression and move through that very "dark" period. At one point, due to a job layoff, he reported wanting to be dead and wishing he could kill himself (but no specific plan or any reported suicidal attempts), as he felt his creativity and hard work ethic were challenged, despite the fact that he did not like the job and wanted to leave it. He denies ever being hospitalized for psychiatric care. He reports difficulty sleeping, so he will watch TV in bed until he can fall asleep. Furthermore, he reports feeling hopeless on a regular basis. He refuses to take psychotropic medications for his depression, and he pays cash so there is no record of him receiving psychological services.

Finally, his faith is a source of comfort to him at times, and he seems to identify more with being culturally, rather than religiously, Jewish. He reports attending synagogue during the

High Holy Days in the fall, as well as services when a person has a bar or bat mitzvah or funeral.

GUIDING QUESTIONS

- What additional theories would you use to work with this client? What specific aspects of those theories do you think are most helpful?
- How would you evaluate the client's progress? How long would you continue to treat a client who makes minor changes in his life, yet states he wants to come to therapy because it is very helpful to him? How would you use the National Association of Social Workers *Code of Ethics* (2017) to guide your approach in this area?
- How would you motivate him to make changes in his life?
- How do you understand how his religion may be a source of support to and resilience for him?
- What referrals would you make to the client? Why would you make the specific referrals?

CASE FORMULATION

Generalist Formulation

Scott, a divorced, gay father of two adult children, grew up in a Jewish home where he was judged and criticized often by family. This has contributed to being very critical of himself and others and cultivating a very low self-esteem and worth (as supported by low scores on self-esteem scales). This stance often affects his interpersonal relationships with other gay men. Scott meets criteria for major depressive disorder, recurrent, as well as persistent depressive disorder.

Culturally Responsive and Queer-Affirmative Formulation

Scott is a fifty-five-year-old gay, white, Jewish man who has experienced verbal, emotional, and psychological abuse from childhood through adulthood by his parents, specifically his mother. In fact, this abuse also has been traumatizing for Scott, compounded by a history of struggling with his sexuality, growing up in a less than affirming environment, forcing himself to get married, and then later negotiating how to disclose. The experience of punitive, abusive relationships has continued into his adulthood as he came out as a gay male and continued to be verbally judged and criticized by other gay men due to his low self-esteem and body habitus. Through these judgments and abuse, he has often felt guilt and shame for who he has been and for what he has done, trying to reconcile these various elements of his identity and relationships.

TREATMENT AND ACTION PLANNING

- *Psychotherapy as a safer and transformative space*: The clinical social worker has and would necessarily continue to provide a supportive, safe, and holding environment for Scott to experience a nonjudgmental space (Brice, 2011). Specifically, the clinician could use both a client-centered and a self-psychology approach (e.g., mirroring, idealization, and twinship). In the course of his long-term treatment, the clinician has often used psychodynamic theories to understand the client, specifically ego psychology and object relations theory, and then used a narrative approach to change how he viewed himself, others, and his life story. The narrative approach allowed the client a place to share his stories to make sense of himself, his actions, and his relationships. To this end, the therapist provides interpretations as to why Scott acts and thinks in the ways he does. Finally, the clinician facilitates a continual linking from past experiences from his family, especially his mother, to his current thoughts and actions. For an effective primer for social workers, see Brandell (2014).

- *The roles of trauma*: Appreciating Scott's case within a traumatic stress frame can be a generative way to give more comprehensive attention to his situation. The continued presence of Scott's long-term childhood experiences in his present life and conflicts merits further exploration in the course of therapy. Appreciating his current behavior and quality of life from this standpoint would also offer space to consider the ways in which his history of traumatic experiences contributes to current risk and resilience (Balcom, 2000; Burnham et al., 2016; Rosenberg, 2000; van der Kolk, 2015; Yu, Chen, Ye, Li, & Lin, 2017).

- *Intimacy*: Furthermore, an important part of the therapeutic process would be for Scott to work on decreasing his self-judgment and other judgments so that he can work on developing a support system, increasing his socializing, and deepening his capacity for and experience of platonic and romantic intimacy (Coren, 2015).

- *Safety and security*: At one point in treatment, Scott became so depressed that he experienced suicidal ideation for several months. That period underscored the need to consistently assess for suicidality, per routine standards. However, given the veracity of those thoughts, Scott and the clinical social worker brought to the forefront the need for a "first aid" kit and more concrete and active suicide prevention plans (as inspired by dialectical behavior therapy; Linehan, 2014).

■ *HIV treatment, prevention, and disclosure*: Finally, related to the safety issue above, another area for continued exploration with Scott is that of his HIV status and management of risk and transmission. His adherence to antiretroviral medications is an effective strategy for not only maintaining his health but also reducing transmission of the virus to sexual partners. (For further information on treatment as prevention, see https://www .cdc.gov/hiv/risk/art.) Part of this sex-positive and HIV-affirmative conversation would be attention to risk and prevention around other sexually transmitted infections, as antiretroviral medications do not prevent or protect against other viruses and bacteria. Equally salient is a discussion about how to disclose Scott's HIV status to prospective partners, as well as their options for prevention and reducing risk during sexual encounters, including partners taking PrEP, or preexposure prophylaxis (see https://www.cdc.gov/hiv/risk/prep).

REFERENCES AND RESOURCES

Balcom, D. (2000). Eye movement desensitization and reprocessing in the treatment of traumatized gay men. *Journal of Gay & Lesbian Social Services, 12*(1–2), 75–89.

Brandell, J. R. (Ed.). (2014). *Essentials of clinical social work.* Los Angeles, CA: Sage.

Brice, A. (2011). "If I go back, they'll kill me . . .": Person-centered therapy with lesbian and gay clients. *Person-Centered and Experiential Psychotherapies, 10*(4), 248–259.

Burnham, K. E., Cruess, D. G., Kalichman, M. O., Grebler, T., Cherry, C., & Kalichman, S. C. (2016). Trauma symptoms, internalized stigma, social support, and sexual risk behavior among HIV-positive gay and bisexual MSM who have sought sex partners online. *AIDS Care, 28*(3), 347–353.

Coren, S. (2015). Understanding and using enactments to further clinical work: A case study of a man unable to experience intimacy. *Journal of Clinical Psychology, 71*(5), 478–490.

Kantor, M. (1999). *Treating emotional disorder in gay men.* Westport, CT: Praeger.

Linehan, M. (2014). *DBT skills training handouts and worksheets* (2nd ed.). New York, NY: Guilford Press.

National Association of Social Workers. (2017). *Code of ethics of the National Association of Social Workers.* Washington, DC: Author.

Rosenberg, L. G. (2000). Phase oriented psychotherapy for gay men recovering from trauma. *Journal of Gay & Lesbian Social Services, 12*(1/2), 37–73.

van der Kolk, B. (2015). *The body keeps the score: Brain, mind, and body in the healing of trauma.* New York, NY: Penguin.

Yu, N. X., Chen, L., Ye, Z., Li, X., & Lin, D. (2017). Impacts of making sense of adversity on depression, posttraumatic stress disorder, and posttraumatic growth among a sample of mainly newly diagnosed HIV-positive Chinese young homosexual men: The mediating role of resilience. *AIDS Care, 29*(1), 79–85.

11

A GOOD CHRISTIAN MAN

TERRENCE O. LEWIS

Marcus self-identifies as a twenty-two-year-old, African American, single, gay, cisgender man. Recently, he graduated with a BA in religious studies from a prestigious university in Boston. Following the recommendation of a close friend, Marcus set up a counseling appointment at a community mental health center's adult outpatient program. During the initial phone conversation with the intake department, he disclosed that he was experiencing "significant anxiety over the past month." He denied suicidal ideation; however, he did state that his friends were "really worried" about him.

Marcus arrived early for his first appointment with the clinical social worker. He was dressed in business casual and age-appropriate attire (e.g., dress slacks, collared shirt with rolled-up sleeves). He presented as friendly with blunted affect and dysphoric mood. Marcus stated that he was familiar with the process of therapy because he met briefly with a counselor during his freshman year of college, when he about eighteen years old. He stated that the counselor was supportive; however, he wished that she was more helpful regarding his questions about sexual orientation. He stated that he struggled with same-sex attraction due to his strong religious values and upbringing in a traditional black Baptist church in Georgia. Still, he took the step to come out as a gay man last year.

Marcus leaned forward in his chair and looked at the floor as he spoke about his coming-out process. He shared that he always felt different, yet he didn't "have the words to describe the difference" until he was in high school. Marcus developed "strong feelings" for his best friend, Leo. Marcus stated, "I felt weird and goofy around Leo, that butterflies in your stomach feeling. I even dreamt about kissing him. The feelings freaked me out!" Leo and Marcus grew up together in the church. From birth to high school graduation, their families celebrated their milestones together in the church. Marcus was raised in a two-parent home in the suburbs of Atlanta. He stated that he was the middle child and only son out of five children. He described his father as a "great dad" who took seriously his duties to raise a "good Christian man" in the African American community. For the most of their lives, Marcus's dad has been a deacon, and Leo's dad had been the senior pastor. Both their mothers were on the usher board and in the choir. Marcus emphasized that the church was "the center of our world." Marcus shared that he showed an aptitude for biblical studies, ministry, and oration at a young age. He stated that he was allowed to give sermons for the special children's Sunday services and, "It was clear to everyone that I was destined to become a minister." Marcus stated he was raised to believe that homosexuality was "an abomination before God." He recounted a painful yet common sermon refrain, "God created Adam and Eve, not Adam and Steve," and Marcus recalled his father's rants about gay people, especially during summer when the local news would cover gay pride events. When Marcus moved to Boston for college, Leo withdrew from him and limited his contact. Marcus stated that he loved Leo; however, he never told him because "that would have destroyed everything." Marcus stated that one of his greatest fears was "disappointing and shaming" his family.

Marcus reported that he started experiencing the following symptoms about one month ago (i.e., a week before graduation): restlessness, decreased sleep, vivid nightmares, decreased appetite, brief anxiety attacks, problems concentrating, and excessive worry about his future. He denied any history of suicidal ideation and substance abuse. Marcus was oriented to person, place, time, and purpose of the counseling session. He denied any symptoms of psychotic process and reported no issues with his memory. Regarding concentration problems, he said, "I have too many thoughts racing through my mind sometimes. It's kind of overwhelming." He stated that most of the thoughts were about his family, his future as a minister, "lack of a love life," and fears about shaming his family. He stated that he experienced similar symptoms in his freshman year when he was struggling with coming out; now, the feelings were more intense. He stated that his friends were worried because he "freaked out" at a party after graduation. He said that he felt overwhelmed about his future after graduation and the reality that he agreed to return home and work as a minister in his old church. During the party, his mind was filled with thoughts about what his parents and minister would say if they were at the party and saw who he "really is." When his anxiety and negative thoughts overwhelmed him, he yelled at his friend for "acting over the top gay" at the party, and then he stormed out. Most of his college friends identified as members of the LGBTQIA community or were straight allies. They were shocked by his behavior at the party. He apologized to them later and tearfully expressed fear of his parents finding out that he is gay. His friends supportively listened to him and encouraged him to reconsider his decision to move back to Georgia. However, Marcus stated that he could not break his promise to his church and family.

Marcus stated that his parents and the pastor (Leo's dad) came to the graduation ceremony. His pastor said that Leo was planning to come to his graduation but could not as he was busy with wedding planning. That was the first time that Marcus heard Leo was getting married to a woman. The pastor came with a gift and a job offer for him. He offered Marcus a position as an associate minister at his home church. Marcus accepted the position and promised his parents that he would return home by the end of the summer. "It is my dream job to serve the community as a minister," stated Marcus, "how could I refuse a job offer from my home church?"

GUIDING QUESTIONS

- What are your beliefs, attitudes, and values regarding LGBTQ+ individuals and their families?
- What are some local and national resources that provide education and training in culturally competent social work practice with LGBTQ+ individuals and their families?
- On a scale of 1 (no LGBT cultural competence) to 10 (exceptional LGBT cultural competence), how would you rate yourself, your teachers, and your social work student peers? How would you rate your family and community?
- Considering intersectionality and critical race theory, what conflicts may exist between Marcus's religious identity, ethnic identity, and sexual orientation?
- How would you assist Marcus in resolving his decision to move back home and work for the church with his gay identity that is not accepted by family and friends?

- How might Marcus's internalized homophobia affect his decision to move back home?
- Does Marcus have friends/supports who identify as LGBTQ+? How might these people affect his decision?

CASE FORMULATION

Generalist Formulation

Marcus reported symptoms that are consistent with a *DSM-5* diagnosis of adjustment disorder with anxiety. His current symptoms and history do not meet the criteria for another mental disorder. While his friends expressed significant concern about his emotional state, Marcus denied thoughts of harming himself or others. He has denied substance abuse, as well. His symptoms appear to be connected to his fears about his family discovering that he is gay. As he stated, he is afraid of "disappointing and shaming" his family.

Culturally Responsive and Queer-Affirmative Formulation

Marcus is an African American, single, cisgender man of Christian faith who claimed his identity as a gay male only one year ago. Marcus expressed the importance of family, faith, and heterosexuality in his socialization narratives of his childhood and adolescence. There is significant emotional and cognitive dissonance between the heterosexual identity that he presents to his family of origin and the gay identity that he shares with his friends and community in Boston. In addition to these conflicts, Marcus has experienced significant homophobic messaging at his "home" church and from his father. His emotional distress and anxiety-related symptoms are expressions of the unresolved tensions between his intersecting identities and the homophobic and heteronormative narrative of his family and home faith community.

FURTHER POLICY INTERSECTIONS

The National Association of Social Workers (2015) published *Standards and Indicators for Cultural Competence in Social Work Practice.* The ten standards emphasize the integral role of cultural competence to every aspect of social work practice, including the following:

- Standard 2: Self-awareness
- Standard 3: Cross-cultural knowledge
- Standard 4: Cross-cultural skills
- Standard 6: Empowerment and advocacy
- Standard 8: Professional education
- Standard 10: Leadership to advance cultural competence

TREATMENT AND ACTION PLANNING

- Social work scholars have developed practice theories and approaches for LGBTQ-affirmative social work practice (Alessi, 2014; Morrow & Messinger, 2006). LGBTQ-affirmative practice starts with the social worker's development of cultural competence. In this case, an LGBTQ-affirmative practice process would include the following elements:

- *Social worker cultural competence self-assessment and training*: Social workers should:
  - ○ Assess their beliefs, values, and biases regarding LGBTQ+ individuals—specifically, nonheterosexual sexual orientations, nonbinary gender identities, and nonconforming gender expressions
  - ○ Seek out culturally rooted knowledge about the lives, strengths, and challenges of LGBTQ+ individuals, their families, and communities
  - ○ Seek out evidence-based LGBTQ+ affirming theories and practice approaches
- *Build LGBTQ+ affirmative rapport with the client*: Social workers should focus on creating a trusting and safe working alliance with LGBTQ+ clients. This process would include:
  - ○ Assessing the work environment for visually affirming and nonaffirming symbols
  - ○ Learning and using LGBTQ+ affirming and nonheteronormative language in written and oral communication
  - ○ Consistent expression of genuine positive regard, nonjudgmental stance, and recognition of client strengths
- *Collaborative multitiered assessment*: Social workers need to facilitate an assessment process that carefully considers the influence of stigma, oppression, and multiple marginalized identities on the client's health and well-being. The assessment would include both a bio-psychosocial-spiritual assessment (Cooper & Lesser, 2011) as well as an assessment of minority stress (Alessi, 2014).

- *Collaborative treatment planning*: In accordance with LGBTQ+ affirmative practice approaches above, a clinical treatment plan for Marcus may include the following interventions:

- *Psychoeducation and skill building to address anxiety symptoms*: The clinician would focus efforts on teaching and practicing mindfulness-based stress reduction exercises with Marcus (Bourne, 2015).

- *Psychotherapy to decrease emotional distress*: Using a combination of cognitive-behavioral and narrative therapies (Cooper & Lesser, 2011; Nichols, 2010), the clinician will work with Marcus to:
  o Critically explore his life narrative as an African American, a Christian, and a gay male and, within his life narrative, identify homophobic and heterosexist messages and experiences
  o Map the influence of homophobic and heterosexist messages and experiences (from his family, home church, the African American community) on his identity development and his current bio-psychosocial-spiritual functioning
  o Use cognitive restructuring and externalizing conversations, help Marcus to diffuse the oppressive messages, and restory his life narrative to affirm his full identity
  o Reassess his decision to move back to Atlanta and join the ministry team at his home church, weigh the pros and cons of the decision, and, if it is his final decision, discuss ways to nurture his full identity, to combat homophobia, and to build a LGBTQ+ affirmative support system

- *Referrals for LGBTQ+ supportive resources*: Using an ecomap, the therapist and Marcus can assess his relational supports and community networks, as well as identify helpful referrals for LGBTQ+ affirmative supports, in Boston and Atlanta. These referrals may include LGBTQ+ affirmative churches in Atlanta.

RESOURCES

Center for LGBTQ and Gender Studies in Religion: https://clgs.org/
The Fellowship: http://www.radicallyinclusive.com/
Human Rights Campaign, Resources for Communities of Color: http://www
.hrc.org/resources/topic/communities-of-color
NASW National Committee on Lesbian, Gay, Bisexual and Transgender
Issues: http://www.socialworkers.org/governance/cmtes/nclgbi.asp
National Black Justice Coalition: http://nbjc.org/
Parents and Friends of Lesbians and Gays (PFLAG): https://www.pflag.org/

REFERENCES

Alessi, E. J. (2014). A framework for incorporating minority stress theory
into treatment with sexual minority clients. *Journal of Gay and Lesbian
Mental Health, 18,* 47–66.

Bourne, E. J. (2015). *The anxiety and phobias workbook.* Oakland, CA: New
Harbinger.

Cooper, M. G., & Lesser, J. G. (2011). *Clinical social work practice: An integrated approach* (4th ed.). Boston, MA: Allyn & Bacon.

Morrow, D. F., & Messinger, L. (Eds.). (2006). *Sexual orientation and gender expression in social work practice.* New York, NY: Columbia University Press.

National Association of Social Workers. (2015). *Standards and indicators for
cultural competence in social work practice.* Washington, DC: NASW Press.

Nichols, M. P. (2010). *Family therapy concepts and methods* (9th ed.). Boston,
MA: Allyn & Bacon.

12

AGING OUT

SARAH MOUNTZ

S asha is a nineteen-year-old, bilingual, transgender, heterosexual-identified woman who was placed, three years ago, in foster care on a person in need of supervision (PINS) petition by her grandparents. Until the age of nine, Sasha was primarily raised by her single mother in Puerto Rico, who has had and continues to have struggles with alcohol and other drugs. Due to those struggles, Sasha's maternal grandparents petitioned for her to relocate to New York City from Puerto Rico, where they had been living for six years at that point so they could be closer to their other daughter, Sasha's aunt. While her grandparents had only been around in Puerto Rico for the first few years of Sasha's life, Sasha always held a special place in their hearts. Sasha's mother agreed to the move, and Sasha moved to the Bronx, experiencing a largely smooth transition into her grandparents' home. Sasha began school in New York, found the subway and the city lights thrilling, and experienced relief from her prior life with her mom by enjoying the relative stability of her grandparents' home. Still, in the initial years in New York, Sasha often felt a sting of betrayal about her mother seeming to have chosen drugs over her; in kind, she would sometimes pick fights with her cousins, who had become veritable siblings as they lived closed and socialized often. Also, Sasha often voiced worry to her grandparents about her mother's health and well-being.

While assigned male at birth, for most of her life, Sasha preferred clothing and colors that her grandparents considered "feminine," and she grew her hair long. As early as five years old, Sasha felt very clear that she identified with girls in the television programs she watched and that she knew that she was a girl, all the while not sharing this with anyone else. Sasha's grandparents subtly noted their disapproval of her intermittent moments of feminine presentation, chiding her about her choice of hairstyle and suggesting she was too "soft." As she entered adolescence, their admonishments became bigger and often escalated into yelling. All the while, Sasha's desire to express her feminine gender identity grew stronger and stronger. Sasha's grandparents did not approve of her more feminine attire, and so she would leave for school wearing the clothes they had purchased for her, bringing a different outfit to change into on the way to school.

Around the time Sasha turned fifteen, she began missing school and staying out late, not letting her grandparents know where she was. When she started being truant chronically, her grandparents would confront her after the school called, and arguments would ensue, even to the point that Sasha started to curse out her grandma directly. After about a year of these conflicts, at sixteen years old, things reached a boiling point for Sasha. Her grandmother walked in on Sasha in her bedroom wearing one of her cousin's dresses, at which point her grandmother began furiously hitting Sasha and calling her *maricon* (faggot). When she escaped her grandmother's grasp, Sasha pushed her out of the room, packed a bag, and left the apartment. That night, Sasha stayed at a friend's house and thereafter couch surfed with other friends. Simultaneously, within the next few days, Sasha's grandmother went to the Bronx family court to file a PINS petition, which resulted in Sasha being placed in foster care.

Still not even seventeen, Sasha was first placed in a congregate care facility for boys. She was verbally harassed and physically threatened by some of the other residents in the house. Many of the line staff misgendered her, referring to Sasha as "he" and calling her by her "dead name," that is, the name given to her at birth. In addition, she was only allowed to purchase male clothing; without recourse to advocate effectively for herself at that point, she began shoplifting. After having been caught shoplifting several times at Forever 21, Sasha was tried and sent to a juvenile justice facility in New York for six months. Upon her release, her Administration for Children Services caseworker placed her in a specialized congregate care facility for LGBTQ+ youth in the foster care system, where she currently resides.

Turning to the present moment, in a couple weeks, Sasha turns twenty—leaving her with one year until she ages out of foster care. Her agency-based caseworker, Damian, has been working with her on a transition plan, but he is dissatisfied that Sasha does not have a GED or legal employment. Sasha dropped out of high school after returning from detention; at that point, she was far behind in her credits toward graduation and did not feel like she could catch up in a timely manner. Before leaving school, Sasha really enjoyed and did well in biology and English. Her decision not to go back to school was also informed by the fact that she had previously experienced a hostile school climate. While in school, Sasha regularly experienced both interpersonal bullying by peers and a hostile school climate due to policies such as being denied access to girls' restrooms and locker rooms.

Instead of attending school, Sasha has filled her time with a variety of developing interests and hobbies related to her passions:

fashion, dancing, and performing. Over the past year and a half, since leaving detention, Sasha has become very connected to the ballroom community in New York City. In particular, she is part of the House of Fantasia, who she considers her family now; incidentally, since her placement in the foster care system, Sasha has not had communication with her biological family. Also, in the past two years, Sasha has developed a best friend relationship with Trina, another young trans woman who lives in her group home.

Recently, when her caseworker, Damian, questioned Sasha about her educational and employment plans for the future, she shared that she participates in the underground economy in various ways to have the funds to access silicon injections and hormone treatment from a street provider. She learned of this system from her peers, who also taught her how to self-administer the hormones. Since becoming involved in the House of Fantasia, her house mother has begun talking to her about the importance of safe injection and urging her to speak with Damian about finding a licensed medical provider to oversee her treatment. Her house father has also encouraged her to pursue her GED and then community college, as well as offered to connect her to an LGBTQ+ youth-serving HIV prevention program in the city that offers paid internships for young people. Up to this point, Sasha's house parents and Damian have not met or communicated with each other, despite sharing aspirations for and an investment in Sasha. Finally, as of late, Sasha has been returning to the group home past curfew, high on marijuana and intoxicated, and she has shared with Damian that she feels "lost between worlds," referring to her highly institutionalized existence within the group home and her more freeing and affirming experience of family life and performance within the ballroom community.

GUIDING QUESTIONS

- What other information would be helpful in your assessment, particularly focusing on the impending aging out of the foster system?
- How do we make sense of this situation? What about making sense from the standpoints of Sasha, Sasha's grandparents, the child welfare system, Sasha's caseworker, and/or Sasha's ballroom family?
- Which clinical models or approaches might be helpful here to unpack this situation as well as shed light on processing the struggles this individual is facing?
- How might you work to establish permanency for Sasha as she transitions out of foster care? What housing options may be available to Sasha after leaving foster care?
- What developmental considerations should be taken into account? What medical and health considerations should be made?
- What forms of trauma may have Sasha experienced or currently be experiencing, and in what ways could you work in a trauma-informed manner? What would trauma-informed care look like at the micro, mezzo, and macro levels?

CASE FORMULATION

Generalist Formulation

This nineteen-year-old Puerto Rican transgender woman has been "kicked out" of her home and is now residing in the foster care system. A "crossover youth," she has a history of juvenile justice involvement and limited education, both of which may get in the way of her gaining employment and achieving stable housing and social connections after transitioning from foster care. She is currently engaging in activities, such as substance use and participation in underground economies, which place her at increased risk for HIV infection and other sexually transmitted infections and negative health outcomes.

Culturally Responsive and Queer-Affirmative Formulation

Sasha is a trans woman of color who has been surviving in the matrix of intersecting racism, classism, adultism, and transphobia. In response, she has had to navigate the criminalization of her identities over the course of her young life, starting with the disapprovals from her grandparents and then social policing by her peers in school and neglect by the school. Then, Sasha has experienced involvement in both the child welfare and juvenile justice systems, locations wherein young queer and trans people of color (QTPOC) are disproportionately represented (Irvine & Canfield, 2016; Wilson & Kastanis, 2015). In response, Sasha has engaged in survival strategies so common to young QTPOC.

Her kinship care placement was interrupted by her grandparents' rejection of Sasha's gender identity and expression, posing a threat to her permanency and housing stability in adulthood. Institutionalization of the gender binary (i.e., distinct, binary, inflexible systems for girls and boys) has also contributed to Sasha's experience of an initial nonaffirming congregate care placement within the child welfare system. In kind, this hostile climate blocked her access to gender-affirming prevention and care (e.g., restrooms, locker rooms, medical care). Despite these barriers, Sasha has survived in a world that is hostile toward her identities. She has formed supportive relationships with a chosen kinship network (e.g., the ballroom community), in which she experiences familial connections and peer support. This affirming community facilitates her talent and love for dance, and Sasha is able to spend considerable time in a space where her multiple and intersecting identities are nourished, rather than policed, erased, and denied.

TREATMENT AND ACTION PLANNING

- *Clinician reflexivity*: In a case such as this, the social worker should initiate practice from a place of reflexivity with consideration for their own personal history and social identities in relation to those of Sasha. These identities and histories can show up in various relationship dynamics in practice and therefore should be named and acknowledged where appropriate. This includes consideration of race and ethnicity, sexual orientation and gender identity, class and educational backgrounds, citizenship status, HIV status, and experiences of diaspora, among others. In addition, it is important for the practitioner to unpack personal and societal assumptions and ideologies regarding "family" and kinship, as they relate to the intersections of culture, child welfare history (or lack thereof), sexual orientation, and gender identity. "Chosen family" or "fictive kin" established outside of blood or genetic relations often have particular bearing in the lives of child welfare–involved LGBTQ+ young people (Arnold & Bailey, 2009; Mallon & DeCrescenzo, 2006).
- *Relational permanency planning*: Beyond simply considering her legal permanency upon aging out of foster care at twenty-one,

the social worker should work with Sasha and others involved in her case to explore relational permanency. This means consideration for both formal and informal adult relationships Sasha sees as central to her life, some of whom she may call upon as sustainable sources of support as she transitions out of the foster care system (Samuels, 2008). In collaboration with her child welfare agency-based caseworker, the social worker should have ongoing conversations with Sasha to identify these relationships and build on them. Specifically, it would be worthwhile to draw on the considerable support she receives via her family within the House of Fantasia. Should Sasha be amenable, it may be effective to bring Sasha's house parents into her planning for the future, specifically in the areas in which they have already proven supportive: providing education about safer sex and HIV testing, encouraging educational and employment aspirations, and providing ongoing social support and a sense of belonging.

Likewise, further engagement with Sasha's grandparents will allow the social worker to assess where they are on the caregiver spectrum of acceptance and rejection. There is often room for movement toward greater acceptance when using the family acceptance project model (Ryan, 2009); this would be predicated upon Sasha being open to a family-based intervention and her grandparents evidencing increased acceptance. The clinician may also wish to explore relationship possibilities with other members of Sasha's family of origin, including any other extended family members who may reside in New York and Sasha's birth mother and other family members in Puerto Rico. The clinician will first need to assess the safety and stability of these family members, especially with regard to levels of acceptance of Sasha's gender identity.

Ultimately, the social worker can engage those people whom Sasha has identified as family or permanency resources using a wraparound service model that centers youth and family in a process of collaborative planning (Walker & Baird, 2019).

■ *Facilitating safe medical transition*: Although Sasha has a history of securing gender-affirming hormones through the underground economy, recent changes in New York State Medicaid policy make her eligible for coverage through a medical provider. The social worker should connect Sasha to a gender-affirming medical provider who can provide ongoing maintenance of an indicated protocol for her medical transition. To access hormone treatment and other medical procedures related to a gender-affirming medical transition, Sasha will need access to a licensed therapist who can support her in navigating her process vis-à-vis the normative and hostile world; this would invariably involve a clinician who provides necessary documentation related to medical transition in accordance with the World Professional Association for Transgender Health and the Standards of Care (www.wpath.org) and is skilled in trans-affirming practice with young people, such as the gender-affirmative model (Keio-Meyer & Ehrensaft, 2018). The clinician should operate from a framework of intersectional consciousness that takes into consideration Sasha's multiple intersecting marginalized identities along various axes of power, privilege, and oppression (Crenshaw, 1997).

The clinician should also be attentive to the considerable safety concerns young trans women of color must face, as well as the varied and complex forms of trauma trans women of color often survive over the course of their lives, which may take the form of bullying, family rejection, street harassment, sexual abuse and assault, and state-sanctioned violence, among others (Keio-Meyer & Ehrensaft, 2018; Mountz, 2016; Singh,

2011; Stotzer, 2009). Given these experiences, a trauma-informed approach is imperative and one that integrates gender-affirming safety planning, such as the Inclusive Safety Plan of Care for transgender youth of color (Ashley, Lipscomb, & Mountz, in press). In addition, there should be at least an equal focus on resilience, strengths, and the ways in which Sasha has survived in a world that is hostile toward her identities and existence (Singh, 2018). Finally, therapy with Sasha should approach her current substance use by using a harm reduction approach that takes into consideration Sasha's desire and willingness to stop or reduce drug and alcohol use. A harm reduction approach might explore the ways in which substance use over time could interfere with Sasha's current and future housing possibilities and other aspirations or might place her at increased risk for criminal (in)justice involvement or poor health outcomes (Marlatt, 1998). If Sasha has a desire to engage in treatment, a suggested model for working with her co-occurring substance use and trauma survivorship is the seeking safety model, an evidence-based, present-focused treatment model that can occur individually or in groups (Najavits, 2009).

- *Activism, empowerment, and consciousness raising*: If she is not already connected to them, Sasha may benefit from engaging with community activist groups led by her peers. Several such groups are committed to building the community capacity of young QTPOC in New York City. Groups like Fierce (http://fiercenyc.org/) and the Audre Lorde Project (https://alp.org/) work to advocate for expanded resources and to change policies that result in the criminalization of QTPOC communities and "pipelines" that contribute to their disproportionate representation in criminal (in)justice systems. In addition, Sasha may

wish to engage in social change work with other members of
the Puerto Rican community specifically and could be connected, for example, to the Puerto Rican Initiative to Develop
Empowerment (www.prideny.com).

■ *Housing*: Housing options for youth exiting foster care remain
limited, as evidenced by the fact than 25 percent of youth exiting the foster care system experience homelessness within two
to four years of aging out (https://www.covenanthouse.org
/homeless-teen-issues/statistics). Although there are no statis-
tical data, exploratory research projects show that the rates are
even higher among transgender former foster youth (Mountz,
Capous-Desyllas, & Pourciau, 2018). For trans former foster
youth specifically, housing options may be further restricted
by caregiver and worker bias and discrimination, gender-
segregated transitional housing facilities and other residential
options, employment discrimination, and rejection by family of
origin, extended family, and foster caregivers (Mountz et al.,
2018). Although beds within these facilities are limited, there
are a few queer- and trans-affirming longer-term housing options for transitional aged youth in New York City, including
the True Color residences (http://westendres.org/residences
/true-colors-bronx/), the Chelsea Foyer (https://goodshepherds
.org/program/chelsea-foyer/), and the Door's Supportive Housing program (https://door.org/programs-services/supportive
-housing/). Other options for youth aging out of foster care
include Section 8 vouchers or applying to live in public housing. The social worker should work collaboratively with Sasha
to determine the safest and most feasible housing options for
her, as well as work with her to submit applications well in
advance of her twenty-first birthday because of the general
shortage of safe and affordable housing options.

RESOURCES

Gaskin, G. H. (2013). *Legendary: Inside the house ballroom scene.* Durham, NC: Duke University Press.

Johnson, S. D., Bratton, E., Dobson, D., Leidner, N. E., Smith, S., Moretti, E., & Jonze, S. (Executive Producers). (2018). *My house* [Television series]. New York: Viceland.

Livingston, J., Swimar, B. (Producers), & Livingston, J. (Director). (1990). *Paris is burning* [Motion picture]. N.p.: Off White Productions.

Murphy, R., Falchuk, B., Jacobson, N., Simpson, B., Woodall, A. M., & Marsh, S. (Executive Producers). (2018). *Pose* [Television series]. New York, NY: FX Productions.

Renault, C., & Baker, S. (2011). *Voguing and the house ballroom scene of New York City 1989–92.* London, UK: Soul Jazz Books.

REFERENCES

Arnold, E. A., & Bailey, M. M. (2009). Constructing home and family: How the ballroom community supports African American GLBTQ youth in the face of HIV/AIDS. *Journal of Gay & Lesbian Social Services, 21*(2–3), 171–188.

Ashley, W., Lipscomb, A., & Mountz, S. (in press). A toolkit for collaborative safety and treatment planning with transgender youth of color. In *The therapists' notebook for sexual and gender identity diverse clients.* New York, NY: Harrington Park Press.

Crenshaw, K. (1997). Intersectionality and identity politics: Learning from violence against women of color. In M. Lyndon Shanley & U. Narayan (Eds.), *Reconstructing political theory* (pp. 178–193). University Park: Pennsylvania State University Press.

Irvine, A., & Canfield, A. (2016). The overrepresentation of lesbian, gay, bisexual, questioning, gender nonconforming and transgender youth within the child welfare to juvenile justice crossover population. *Journal of Gender, Social Policy & the Law, 24*(2), 243–261.

Keio-Meier, C., & Ehrensaft, D. (Eds.). (2018). *The gender affirmative model: An interdisciplinary approach to supporting transgender and gender expansive children.* Washington, DC: American Psychological Association.

Mallon, G., & De Crescenzo, T. (2006). Transgender children and youth: A child welfare practice perspective. *Child Welfare: Journal of Policy, Practice, and Program, 85*(2), 215–241.

Marlatt, G. A. (1998). *Harm reduction: Pragmatic strategies for managing high risk behavior.* New York, NY: Guilford Press.

Mountz, S. (2016). That's the sound of the police: State sanctioned violence and resistance among LGBTQ young adults previously incarcerated in girls' juvenile justice facilities. *Affilia, 31*(3), 287–302.

Mountz, S., Capous-Desyllas, M., & Pourciau, E. (2018). "Because we're fighting to be ourselves": Voices from transgender and gender expansive former foster youth. *Child Welfare, 96*(1), 103–125.

Najavits, L. M. (2009). Seeking safety: An implementation guide. In A. Rubin & D. W. Springer (Eds.), *The clinician's guide to evidence-based practice* (pp. 311–347). Hoboken, NJ: Wiley.

Ryan, C. (2009). *Supportive families, healthy children: Helping families with lesbian, gay, bisexual and transgender children.* Retrieved from http://nccc .georgetown.edu/documents/LGBT_Brief.pdf

Samuels, G. M. (2008). *A reason, a season, or a lifetime: Relational permanence among young adults with foster care backgrounds.* Chicago, IL: Chapin Hall, Center for Children at the University of Chicago.

Singh, A. A. (2018). *The queer and transgender resilience workbook: Skills for navigating sexual orientation and gender expression.* Oakland, CA: New Harbinger.

Stotzer, R. L. (2009). Violence against transgender people: A review of United States data. *Aggression and Violent Behavior, 14*(3), 170–179.

Walker, J. S., & Baird, C. (2019). *Wraparound for older youth and young adults: Providers' views on whether and how to adapt Wraparound.* Portland, OR: National Wraparound Initiative and Research and Training Center on Pathways to Positive Futures.

Wilson, B. D. M., & Kastanis, A. A. (2015). Sexual and gender minority disproportionality and disparities in child welfare: A population-based study. *Children and Youth Services Review, 58*, 11–17.

13

SUDDENLY STIGMATIZED

JOANNA LA TORRE AND TYLER M. ARGÜELLO

Ivory, a sixteen-year-old, white, cisgender young woman, is reentering the foster system due to her status as a commercially sexually exploited youth (CSEY). Ivory was missing from her foster home for six months, during which time she was held captive by a trafficker, who exploited her physically and emotionally, including beating, raping, and forcibly keeping her on drugs (methamphetamines). During her captivity, Ivory seroconverted as HIV positive and developed many challenging behaviors that contribute to difficulty in finding an appropriate, safe foster placement. When Ivory feels threatened, she externalizes aggressively by yelling, screaming, threatening people, and abusing substances. She also internalizes by cutting herself and shutting down, and she fuses with despondency and para-/suicidality.

A foster home where Ivory had previously been placed has expressed interest in taking her again. Ivory stayed with Judy, a white, cisgender woman, for nearly a year and has expressed interest in returning to the home, citing her strong bond with Judy as well as her two poodles, Germaine and Vincent. Ivory feels excited to get her old room back and to play fetch with "her dogs." Ivory says that Judy and she sometimes argue, but she believes Judy wants to help her. Ivory feels safe when she is with Judy. If placed with Judy, Ivory would be able to return to her former high school where she has friends and knows the teachers, and she could resume counseling with her former therapist.

Judy has provided safe foster homes for teens and young adults for over ten years along with her husband, Bernard, from whom she recently divorced. She has kept in contact with several of her foster kids as they transitioned into adulthood, continuing to invite some of them to her home for events and holidays. Judy shared that she feels a special bond with Ivory and hopes she can make a difference in her life by helping her to become stable. Judy is interested in providing a permanent connection with Ivory, whether it is through long-term foster care, guardianship, or adoption. She is also willing to facilitate and supervise family visitation for Ivory on an ongoing basis, which she has successfully done in the past.

At the child welfare office, during case staffing, the supervisor, Francesca, shared her concerns about Judy's ability to provide a "sexually safe" setting for Ivory. Francesca pointed out that Judy's most recent placement was terminated due to sexual contact between two siblings in her care. Francesca also said she does not feel comfortable now placing Ivory, a youth who has significant sexual trauma, into Judy's home. She states that, shortly after Judy's divorce, Judy's sexuality "suddenly switched" as she is now married to a woman. Francesca said that this change came "out of nowhere," and it makes her feel like Judy is "unpredictable." The team—including Ivory's social worker, a case aide who supervised a visit between Judy and Ivory, and another social worker in training—does not challenge Francesca's concerns.

A decision not to place with Judy would likely lead to Ivory entering a higher level of care, such as a group home, as her behaviors and medical needs exceed the capacity of many foster families. The group homes equipped to work with CSEY are located at least three hours away, which would likely make family visitation infrequent at best.

GUIDING QUESTIONS

- How do ideas about fixed sexuality and/or gender help or hinder culturally competent practice? In what ways are binaries present?
- What assumptions might Francesca be making about Judy and her sexuality? What assumptions might Francesca be making about Bernard's gender and sexuality?
- How do assumptions about gender and sexuality interact with ideas about safety for vulnerable populations?

    - How do you think Francesca's assessment would change if Judy's new spouse was a man? Why?
    - In what ways does perceived change in sexuality become conflated with sexually unsafe or predatory behavior?

- How does trauma inform considerations in formulating the plan for Ivory's care?
- If instead this case were centered on race (e.g., Bernard is white and the new partner is African American), how would Francesca's assumptions and attitudes shift?
- In what ways could or would you intervene to promote cultural competency, and why?

CASE FORMULATION

Generalist Formulation

Ivory is an emotionally and behaviorally disturbed young person. She has a history of several serious traumatic events from her family of origin, as well as after having entered the foster care system. She is both psychiatrically and medically compromised and not well engaged in treatment on either account. Due to the severity and chronicity of her conditions, Ivory is in need of multiple trusted, skilled supports—starting with a competent and enduring foster (to adopt) placement. Whereas Judy has provided a long-standing foster home, there is now concern over her fit with Ivory. In fact, her personal situation causes concern for her own stability as well as that of her household. Whether she has been less than forthcoming with the welfare agency or is new to her current changes, she appears to be in her own process of coming to terms with life stressors. Ivory needs and deserves undivided engagement with and commitment from a foster family. Francesca and the team need to more fully staff this case as well as vet Judy and her home environment.

Culturally Responsive and Queer-Affirmative Formulation

Francesca grew up immersed in societal messages around heteronormativity that problematize ideas of evolving/emerging sexualities and genders, including taking a foundational perspective that they exist on a spectrum. Although she has the best interest of Ivory's safety in mind, her biases are causing her to conflate Judy's sexuality with sexual predation and/or pathology. Her assessment that Judy's sexuality has "suddenly switched" is embedded in the idea that one's sexuality is a fixed, monolithic, and an unchanging attribute of a person that requires careful scrutiny when inconsistent with this notion.

Several explanations exist for Judy's perceived "switch," including the following: the child welfare team never or inadequately included a discussion about sexuality and gender in their assessment and onboarding, Judy identifies as queer and/or bisexual, Judy's sexuality has evolved, Judy just came out of the closet, or Bernard is not a cisgender man. Such explanations account for the perceived discrepancy and do not assign predatory or problematic behavior to a person who has otherwise presented themselves in a trustworthy fashion. Further assessment and/or discussion may provide positive results if sexual safety concerns are able to be ruled out.

Another consideration is the larger agency climate; for example, if one supervisor's biases are being expressed in practice, what other structures (or lack thereof) aid in bias maintenance? The environment in which such attitudes, beliefs, and values are upheld is likely one without adequate discussions, trainings, or attention paid to best practices. Understandings of active or passive biases should be sought to prevent discriminatory actions.

TREATMENT AND ACTION PLANNING

Agencies and large systems of care are sometimes slow to adopt important improvements to services offered and require strategic, well-informed pressure to evolve. This, indeed, is the only way *many* systems have improved to their current state of being, and further efforts will likely see continued advancement. The obstacles in place that prevent the equal treatment of LGBTQ+ individuals and communities require ongoing attention if we are to counteract harms due to pervasive heteronormativity. Advocacy at micro, mezzo, and macro levels is critical to aiding agencies and systems of care in improving understandings of and responsiveness to the LGBTQ+ community. No matter what level of intervention, the paramount concern and focus of action and treatment is the welfare of Ivory, who is at risk of retraumatization and further marginalization, and she is also highly vulnerable psychiatrically and now medically. The plan includes the following:

■ *Case management and referrals*: Ivory is the central focus of this case. To that end, it is important to monitor her symptoms, strengths, and well-being. This work includes:

- Referral to a competent HIV specialty clinic and possibly an AIDS service organization
- If possible, referral to an integrated health clinic that includes HIV specialists, behavioral health, general medical, pharmacy, and education and prevention services, which may mean engagement with a more specialized clinical case management program to follow her throughout these services
- Accompanying Ivory to HIV, medical, and psychiatric appointments
- Adherence work around any prescribed medications in general
- Facilitation of insurance benefits for antiretroviral and other medications, as well as support in adhering to regimens and routine lab work
- Potential referrals to individual as well as group therapy

■ *Trauma-informed care, healing-centered engagement, and affirmative practice*: Ivory has experienced complex trauma, compounded by sexual exploitation, which can be understood as a series of acute traumatic experiences, originating from multiple sources and often manifesting over the trajectory of one's life. These events have the potential to create exponentially negative impacts as the totality of these traumatic experiences can be far more harmful to the development of an individual than the sum of the individual parts (Courtois, 2004; Lawson, Davis, & Brandon, 2013; Wamser-Nanney & Vandenberg, 2013). The impact on neurodevelopment can be long-lasting. Given the severity of the most recent traumas related to sexual exploitation, all services here forward must adhere to standards for CSEY populations (Ijadi-Maghsoodi, Cook, Barnet, Gaboian, & Bath, 2016; Newcombe, 2015; Walker, 2013; Walker & Quraishi, 2015; WestCoast Children's Clinic, 2012):

- Maintain a multidisciplinary team to assess and address Ivory's ongoing treatment needs, including involved parties such as law enforcement/probation, behavioral health, child welfare, and medical providers.
- Use specialized, collaborative, trauma-informed practices in evidence-gathering processes to reduce Ivory's re/traumatization. Have the evidentiary physical examination conducted by a medical provider specially trained in child sexual abuse and have a trusted advocate present during any such procedures. Use a collaborative investigation model (e.g., forensic interviewing), allowing parties involved in legal procedures (e.g., district attorney's office, law enforcement, child welfare) to observe and direct interviews to reduce the number of times victims must retell their stories.

- Make a referral to the Office of Crime Victim's Compensation and ensure Ivory gets enrolled in its services.

- Provide a referral to competent intensive mental health services specializing in stabilization and recovery work with CSEY populations and/or youth with complex trauma.

- Provide support in individually centered activities to promote fun and positive identity development (i.e., manicures, individualized outings, support in completing milestones such as diplomas or employment).

- Promote and maintain healthy long-term connections (e.g., safe family members, former foster parents, previous service providers, previous mentors, appropriate peers), animal-assisted therapy, and provision of nonjudgmental, specialized attention.

- Refer for alcohol and drug treatment services.

■ *Posttraumatic growth (PTG)*: The incidences and ensuing effects of complex trauma are not effectively encased in a framework of pathology. The approach and services offered moving forward for both Ivory and the foster home should also be rooted in empowerment—that is, resilience and PTG. Resilience is often defined as the ability to rebound after a challenge or difficulty, as well as withstand stress through internal and external resources and attributes (Fraser, Richman, & Galinsky, 1999). Social support and community are key to enhancing resilience in vulnerable populations; this begs the attention to re/building the connections with trusted supports, like Judy's home and surrounding community. Related, PTG occurs because of—not despite—traumatic events. PTG can manifest as improvements in personal coping strategies based on lessons emergent from traumatic exposure; finding personal inner strengths and a deeper sense of purpose or meaning to life; arriving at a clearer sense of clearer goals and priorities for one's life; cultivating gratitude and appreciation for life, relationships, and other valued elements; and developing enhanced motivation to give back and help others (Helgeson, Reynolds, & Tomich, 2006; Linley & Joseph, 2004; McElheran et al., 2012; Saakvitne, Tennen, & Affleck, 1998). These elements and qualities could be the foci, certainly, of therapy with Ivory's prior therapist.

- *Interprofessional conduct and supervision*: Present are issues of hierarchy in that Francesca is the supervisor in this scenario, making the intervention complicated for a social worker. Still, the elements present invite pursuing any opportunity to avoid adding to the already heavy burden of trauma Ivory faces. Re/placing her in a familiar home, with a person she already has connection with, could substantially aid in her stabilization. All this said, it is important to discern ways to approach the implicit and explicit biases that Francesca apparently holds. This is not only an ethical mandate of social workers—but most important, it is a matter of social justice and health equity for both Ivory and Judy. Without proper attention and intervention, Francesca is (unwittingly) perpetuating minority stress for Judy and more generally enacting toxic cisheternormativity for Ivory (Alessi, Dillon, & Kim, 2015; Feinstein, Goldfried, & Davila, 2012; Meyer, 2003). Minority stress theory involves the processes of sexual prejudice, stigma, and internationalization. The sexual prejudice includes all negative attitudes toward LGBTQ+ people (Herek, 2000), including assuming members of the LGBTQ+ community suffer from mental illness, are sexually deviant and/or promiscuous, are criminals, and/or are drug and alcohol abusers. This prejudice stigmatizes LGBTQ+ people and informs social interactions, including promulgating negative valuations, invalidating, and discrediting (Teliti, 2015). LGBTQ+ people receive various formations of homo/bi/trans-phobia, disgust, or loathing; the surrounding non-LGBTQ+ people and community can be socialized into and further perpetuate these prejudices, biases, and phobias. Accordingly, LGBTQ+ individuals internalize these phobias, which have harmful effects, and those people enacting these prejudices and stigmas come to institutionalize policies and construct a climate that is discriminatory, depriving LGBTQ+ people basic protections surrounding health, safety, housing, jobs, and public accommodation.

■ *Workplace policies and continuing education*: Related to remediating the professional relationships with Francesca, the social worker is also obligated to initiate a conversation with peers to increase awareness and reduce discrimination of LGBTQ+ clients by individual social workers as well as the larger institution on behalf of which they act. A conversation with superiors, such as Francesca, is an example of a mezzo-level intervention and would be even more effective were they to include trainings for the staff to increase competency. An example of macro-level interventions is creating agencywide policies and procedures for practice with LGBTQ+ individuals and communities. In particular, there are trainings available for the child welfare system (see https://lalgbtcenter.org/rise/lgbtq-training -coaching/lgbtq-training-topics); more generally, cultural competency training should include attention to the following issues, among many others:

   • *Affirmative care*: It is imperative to provide affirmative care for both Judy and Ivory—as the former is part of the case of the welfare agency, and the latter is the putative client. This approach would necessarily proffer knowledge that LGBTQ+

people and their identities are representative of normal variations in sexual and gender identity, thus validating LGBTQ+ identities (Craig, Austin, & Alessi, 2013). Also, this approach recognizes that LGBTQ+ people experience discrimination as a result of living in a homophobic and transphobic society (Craig et al., 2013), which intersects with other prejudices and forms of oppression. Professionals often think in binaries with regard to both sexuality and gender. Often social workers and other professionals have subtle homophobic practices that are unexamined and thus come into play when working with someone who identifies as LGBTQ+. These prejudices, coupled with insufficient knowledge, result in poor service delivery, misdiagnoses, pathologizing, and deprecation (Love, Smith, Lyall, Mullins, & Cohn, 2015). Too often, LGBTQ+ clients end up dissatisfied, not seeking care, omitting critical information for care delivery, and receiving heterosexist and nonempathic attitudes from providers.

- *Lesbian health*: Lesbians have distinct health needs. Practitioners should be aware of these health and social equities, and they do their part to increase health equity and not work to exacerbate them. These inequities include higher rates of mood, anxiety, and substance use disorders, among others (Brittain, Baillargeon, McElroy, Aaron, & Gyurcsik, 2006; Nyitray, Corran, Altman, Chikani, & Negrón, 2006; Poteat, 2012). Some of these needs are tied to structural issues, such as experiences of stress and stigma (Brittain et al., 2006).

- *Coming out*: The "coming-out" process varies for lesbians (and others along the LGBTQ+ rainbow spectrum) and often happens at different developmental stages, not simply in adolescence (Cass, 1979; McCarn & Fassinger, 1996; Parks &

Hughes, 2007). Coming out is not a one-time event; rather, it is a lifelong process that involves multiple moments and situations. More critically, one can refer to a process of "coming in," "inviting in," or "becoming" (cf. Hammoud-Becket, 2007; Walters, Evans-Campbell, Simoni, Ronquillo, & Bhuyan, 2006), which can be sensitive language that more accurately indexes the continual, lifelong process of negotiating multiple social locations and intersecting identities, as well as the cumulative and synergistic effects of stress coping and empowerment, such as for LGBTQ+ people of color.

• *Lesbian parenting*: Children raised by lesbian mothers do not seem to differ from those parented by heterosexuals. Golombok, Spencer, and Rutter (2003) found no significant differences in social and emotional development. Wainwright, Russell, and Patterson (2004) found no difference in self-esteem, anxiety, academic achievement, and peer relationships. Overall, few differences have been shown in the development and mental/health outcomes of children raised in LGBTQ+ households (Ariel & McPherson, 2000; Bos, Knox, van Rijn-van Gelderen, & Gartrell, 2016; Bos, van Valen, & van den Boom, 2003, 2004, 2005; Crouch, McNair, & Waters, 2016; Greenfeld, 2015; Hines, 2006; Perrin et al., 2013; Starks, Newcomb, & Mustanski, 2015). This also holds true for adopted children through the child welfare system (Goldberg, Kinkler, Moyer, & Weber, 2014) and those donor-conceived (Zweifel, 2015). Generally, children in LGBTQ+ households develop well (e.g., temperament, mood, aptitude, coping), their parents contribute beneficially to their mental health, and LGBTQ+ couples show more equity in their roles in the household (Bos et al., 2016; Crouch et al., 2016).

- *LGBTQ+ family formations*: LGBTQ+ relationships and families can often push against hetero- and homonormative visions, biases, and values throughout society, from individuals through institutions. Rather than perceiving these relationships and family formations as threats (and therefore engendering phobias and prejudices, as cited above), they may be regarded as innovative social arrangements, ones that are more inclusive and oriented toward social justice health equity (see, e.g., The Beyond Same-Sex Marriage collective [BSSM, 2008]).

RESOURCES

Alliance for Children's Rights: http://kids-alliance.org/programs/csec/

California Health and Human Services Agency: http://www.chhs.ca.gov /Pages/CAChildWelfareCouncil.aspx

Healing Centered Engagement: https://medium.com/@ginwright/the-fu ture-of-healing-shifting-from-trauma-informed-care-to-healing-centered -engagement-634f557ce69c

Los Angeles LGBT Center, RISE Initiative, including LGBTQ+ affirmative training for child welfare professionals: https://lalgbtcenter.org/rise

National Center for Lesbian Rights: http://www.nclrights.org

The National Center for Youth Law: https://youthlaw.org/case/implementa tion-californias-csec-program/

WestCoast Children's Clinic: http://www.westcoastcc.org/

REFERENCES

Alessi, E. J., Dillon, F. R., & Kim, H. M. (2015). Determinants of lesbian and gay affirmative practice among heterosexual therapists. *Psychotherapy, 52,* 298–307.

Ariel, J., & McPherson, D. W. (2000). Therapy with lesbian and gay parents and their children. *Journal of Marital and Family Therapy, 26*(4), 421–432.

Beyond Same-Sex Marriage (2008). Beyond same-sex marriage: A new strategic vision; Executive summary. *Studies in Gender and Sexuality,* *9*(2), 158–160.

Bos, H. M. W., Knox, J. R., van Rijn-van Gelderen, L., & Gartrell, N. K. (2016). Same-sex and different-sex parent households and child health outcomes: Findings from the National Survey of Children's Health. *Journal of Developmental & Behavioral Pediatrics, 37,* 179–186.

Bos, H. M. W., van Balen, F., & van den Boom, D. C. (2003). Planned lesbian families: Their desire and motivation to have children. *Human Reproduction, 18*(10), 2216–2224.

Bos, H. M. W., van Balen, F., & van den Boom, D. C. (2004). Experience of parenthood, couple relationship, social support, and child-rearing goals in planned lesbian mother families. *Journal of Child Psychology and Psychiatry, 45*(4), 755–764.

Bos, H. M. W., van Balen, F., & van den Boom, D. C. (2005). Lesbian families and family functioning: An overview. *Patient Education and Counseling, 59,* 263–275.

Brittain, D. R., Baillargeon, T., McElroy, M., Aaron, D. J., & Gyurcsik, N. C. (2006). Barriers to moderate physical activity in adult lesbians. *Women Health, 43*(1), 75–92.

Cass, V. C. (1979). Homosexual identity formation: A theoretical model. *Journal of Homosexuality, 4,* 219–235.

Courtois, C. (2004). Complex trauma, complex reactions: Assessment and treatment. *Psychotherapy, Theory, Research, Practice, Training, 41*(4), 412–425.

Craig, S. L., Austin, A., & Alessi, E. (2013). Gay affirmative cognitive behavioral therapy for sexual minority youth: A clinical adaptation. *Journal of Clinical Social Work, 41,* 258–266.

Crouch, S. R., McNair, R., & Waters, E. (2016). Impact of family structure and sociodemographic characteristics on child health and wellbeing in same-sex parent families: A cross-sectional survey. *Journal of Pediatrics and Child Health, 52,* 499–505.

Feinstein, B. A., Goldfried, M. R., & Davila, J. (2012). The relationship between experiences of discrimination and mental health among lesbians and gay men: An examination of internalized homonegativity and rejection sensitivity as potential mechanisms. *Journal of Consulting and Clinical Psychology, 80,* 917–927.

Fraser, M. W., Richman, J. M., & Galinsky, M. J. (1999). Risk, protection, and resilience: Toward a conceptual framework for social work practice. *Social Work Research, 23*(3), 131–143.

Goldberg, A. E., Kinkler, L. A., Moyer, A. M., & Weber, E. (2014). Intimate relationship challenges in early parenthood among lesbian, gay, and heterosexual couples adopting via the child welfare system. *Professional Psychology: Research and Practice, 45*(4), 221–230.

Golombok, S., Spencer, A., & Rutter, M. (2003). Children in lesbian and single-parent households: Psychosexual and psychiatric appraisal. *Journal of Child Psychology and Psychiatry, 24,* 551–572.

Greenfeld, D. A. (2015). Effects and outcomes of third-party reproduction: Parents. *Fertility and Sterility, 104*(3), 520–524.

Hammoud-Becket, S. (2007). *Azima ila hayati*—an invitation in to my life: Narrative conversations about sexual identity. *International Journal of Narrative Therapy and Community Work, 1,* 29–39.

Helgeson, V. S., Reynolds, K. A., & Tomich, P. L. (2006). A meta-analytic review of benefit finding and growth. *Journal of Consulting and Clinical Psychology, 74,* 797–816.

Herek, G. M. (2000). The psychology of sexual prejudice. *Current Directions in Psychological Science, 9,* 19–22.

Hines, S. (2006). Intimate transitions: Transgender practices of partnering and parenting. *Sociology, 40*(2), 353–371.

Ijadi-Maghsoodi, R., Cook, M., Barnet, E. S., Gaboian, S., & Bath, E. (2016). Understanding and responding to the needs of commercially sexually exploited youth: Recommendations for the mental health provider. *Child Adolescent Psychiatric Clinics of North America, 25*(1), 107–122.

Lawson, D., Davis, D., & Brandon, S. (2013). Treating complex trauma: Critical interventions with adults who experiences ongoing trauma in childhood. *Psychotherapy, 50*(3), 331–335.

Linley, P. A., & Joseph, S. (2004). Positive change following trauma and adversity: A review. *Journal of Traumatic Stress, 17*(1), 11–21.

Love, M. M., Smith, A. E., Lyall, S. E., Mullins, J. L., & Cohn, T. J. (2015). Exploring the relationship between gay affirmative practice and empathy among mental health professionals. *Journal of Multicultural Counseling & Development, 43*(2), 83–96.

McCarn, S. R., & Fassinger, R. E. (1996). Re-visioning sexual minority identity formation: A new model of lesbian identity and its implications for counseling and research. *The Counseling Psychologist, 24*(3), 508–534.

McElheran, M., Briscoe-Smith, A., Khaylis, A., Westrup, D., Hayward, C., & Gore-Felton, C. (2012). A conceptual model of post-traumatic growth among children and adolescents in the aftermath of sexual abuse. *Counseling Psychology Quarterly, 25*(1), 73–82.

Meyer, I. H. (2003). Prejudice, social stress, and mental health in lesbian, gay, and bisexual populations: Conceptual issues and research evidence. *Psychological Bulletin, 129,* 674–697.

Newcombe, A. (2015). An advocate's guide to protecting trafficking victims in the child welfare system. *Child Law Practice, 34*(10), 149–157.

Nyitray, A., Corran, R., Altman, K., Chikani, V., & Negrón, E. V. (2006). *Tobacco use and interventions among Arizona lesbian, gay, bisexual and transgender people.* Phoenix: Arizona Department of Health Services. Retrieved from http://www.lgbttobacco.org/files/Arizona_smoking _lgbt_report.pdf

Parks, C., & Hughes, T. L. (2007). Age differences in lesbian identity development and drinking. *Substance Use and Misuse, 42*(2–3), 361–380.

Perrin, E. C., Siegel, B. S., Pawelski, J. G., Dobbins, M. I., Lavin, A., Mattson, G., & Yogman, M. (2013). Promoting the well-being of children whose parents are gay or lesbian. *Pediatrics, 131*(4), e1374–e1383.

Poteat, T. (2012). Top 10 things lesbians should discuss with their healthcare provider. Retrieved from http://www.glma.org/_data/n_0001/resources/ live/Top%2010%20forlesbians.pdf

Saakvitne, K. W., Tennen, H., & Affleck, G. (1998). Exploring thriving in the context of clinical trauma theory: Constructivist self development theory. *Journal of Social Issues, 54*(2), 279–299.

Starks, T. J., Newcomb, M. E., & Mustanski, B. (2015). A longitudinal study of interpersonal relationships among lesbian, gay, and bisexual adolescents and young adults: Mediational pathways from attachment to romantic relationship quality. *Archives of Sexual Behavior, 44,* 1821–1831.

Teliti, A. (2015). Sexual prejudice and stigma of LGBTQ people. *European Scientific Journal, 11*(14), 60–69.

Wainright, J. L., Russell, S. T., & Patterson, C. J. (2004). Psychosocial adjustment, school outcomes, and romantic relationships of adolescents with same-sex parents. *Child Development, 75*(6), 1886–1989.

Walker, K. (2013). Ending the commercial sexual exploitation of children: A call for multi-system collaboration in California. Retrieved from http://www.chhs.ca.gov/Child%20Welfare/Ending%20CSEC%20 -%20A%20Call%20for%20Multi-System%20Collaboration%20in%20 CA%20-%20February%202013.pdf

Walker, K., & Quraishi, F. (2015). *From theory to practice: Creating victim-centered systems of care to address the needs of commercially sexually exploited youth.* Washington, DC: First Focus. Retrieved from https://firstfocus.org /resources/report/from-theory-to-practice-creating-victim-centered -systems-of-care-to-address-the-needs-of-commercially-sexually -exploited-youth

Walters, K. L., Evans-Campbell, T., Simoni, J., Ronquillo, T., & Bhuyan, R. (2006). "My spirit in my heart": Identity experiences and challenges among American Indian two-spirit women. *Journal of Lesbian Studies, 10*(1/2), 125–149.

Wamser-Nanney, R., & Vandenberg, B. (2013). Empirical support for the definition of a complex trauma event in children and adolescents. *Journal of Traumatic Stress, 26*(6), 671–768.

WestCoast Children's Clinic. (2012). *Research to action: Sexually exploited minors (SEM) needs and strengths.* Oakland, CA: WestCoast Children's Clinic.

Zweifel, J. E. (2015). Donor conception from the viewpoint of the child: Positive, negatives, and promoting the welfare of the child. *Fertility and Sterility, 104*(3), 513–519.

14

SAYING GOODBYE

Re-membering Conversations

CHRYSTAL C. RAMIREZ BARRANTI

AND TYLER M. ARGÜELLO

L ark and Holly, legally married for eight years, are a polyamorous couple who came to therapy to address the growing conflict their relationship has been experiencing over the past many months. Lark is a forty-year-old, white, nonbinary trans woman (preferred gender pronouns: they, them, theirs) who is also neurodiverse (i.e., a concept and social movement that advocates for viewing autism spectrum disorder as a variation of human wiring rather than a disease). Lark indicates that they have struggled with depression, anxiety, and panic attacks since adolescence and reports that the depression and anxiety have been more present over the past months. They also indicate that they struggle with insomnia. Lark reports that they have been in therapy in the past and currently take Valium for sleep. Holly, a forty-one-year-old, white, pansexual cisgender female (preferred gender pronouns: she, her, hers), indicates that she too has been struggling with some depression, anxiety, and panic attacks "all of my life" with a recent increase as difficulties in the relationship have emerged. Holly has been prescribed Wellbutrin and is taking it as prescribed. She also reveals a relationship with alcohol (i.e., several glasses of wine every evening) that seems to have increased alongside spending more and more time alone. Both Lark and Holly report that they use marijuana medicinally to relieve anxiety.

Holly has a college education in English literature, while Lark attended some college but did not finish their four-year degree. Both Lark and Holly are employed full-time. Holly describes her work as an administrative assistant to be extremely stressful due to a hostile work environment specifically related to her supervisor. As a result, she reveals that she experiences a sense of failure. Lark has been working for several years as the program coordinator for a grassroots mental health agency that serves the LGBTQI community of a large city on the West Coast. Lark states that their work is extremely fulfilling, although consuming of their energies as they work very long hours. This has kept them away from home well into the late evenings and contributed to exhaustion. In fact, Lark describes the degree of work-related stress this way: "I am working myself quite possibly literally to death."

The couple expresses that they both have been experiencing a great deal of increasing sadness, conflict, anger, and distress over the past months as changes in their relationship have evolved. Both agreed that they have come to therapy wanting help in determining where to go next with their relationship, as it seems that the end or divorce is imminent. Lark stated, "It is difficult to keep going; it is coming to a breaking point with so many stressors," and Holly added tearfully, "Yes, it is difficult to keep going; I am ready to break!"

In response to the clinical social worker's inquiry, "Would it be OK with you two to ask you to share your story of how you first met?," they remarked that the two first met in 2005. It was Lark who first noticed Holly eating in the restaurant where Lark worked. They struck up a conversation and found so many interests in common that they started dating. In 2006, they decided to move in together. Their relationship continued to grow with many affirming qualities. In 2010, with a growing need for Lark to have health insurance, the couple decided to legally marry, notably at that time as an outward-appearing and passing cisheteronormative couple. From early on, the relationship has been consensually nonmonogamous (Moors, Matsick, Ziegler, Rubin, & Conley, 2013), that is, polyamorous, with a shared interest in kink and BDSM (i.e., bondage and discipline, dominance and submission, and sadism and masochism) (Moser & Kleinplatz, 2006). Around 2009–2010, the couple stopped having sex with one another, although the couple continued to share sexual relationships with polyamorous partners.

In 2011, Lark began their transition from male to female bodied. In 2015, they completed their transition with a successful orchiectomy. It is during this time period that Lark and Holly became involved in FetLife, a social networking website that serves people who are interested in BDSM, fetishism, and kink and found a new poly family with a gay couple, Collin and Jack, in 2012. Collin identifies as bisexual in sexual preference while Jack identifies as gay. Jack and Collin are both cisgender males and have been a couple for twenty-plus years.

After Lark's orchiectomy, Holly was more intensely sexually involved with Collin. The polyamorous relationship was initially enriching for both Lark and Holly's own relationship, but the couple noted that they first began to experience stressors in 2016, when Lark invited a temporarily homeless friend (cisgender, neurodiverse female), Lexie, to move in with the couple; then, in 2017, Lark invited her to move in again when she was experiencing despair and suicidality. Lark and Holly's relationship experienced heightened tension as Holly and Lexie did not get along and were involved in frequent arguments. In addition, in April 2017, Collin ended his relationship with Lark, and he and his husband (Jack) remained in a relationship with Holly. Lark expressed that they felt and continue to feel a great deal of sadness and loss over the breakup while also feeling joy in seeing Holly thrive in her relationship with Collin.

Shortly after December 2017, Lark upgraded the couple's computer. In doing so, they unintentionally lost all of Holly's extensive files she had been keeping that documented the couple's relationship, "like when we had our first kiss!" Holly expressed a great deal of anger, sense of loss, and betrayal. Financial stressors also increased during this time and were noted as contributing to a deterioration of trust in one another. The couple has been living in a home owned by Lark's parents with the plan that rent would go toward a purchase of the home. Unexpectedly, Lark's parents have decided they need to sell the home, placing additional stressors on Lark, Holly, and their relationship.

The influence of these critical events on the relationship has initiated the movement of a problem relationship story to the forefront. When the couple was asked, "If I was to interview your relationship, what do you think the relationship would tell me about how it was feeling before the current experiences of distress and upset?" The couple thoughtfully began a remembering conversation. The story of the couple's relationship revealed many foundational values and ethics that grew over the years that they have shared together. In addition to the foundational ethic of "care," the couple identified other core values: "respect for one another," "sharing a group of friends," "common interests such as gaming and card games," "enjoying each other's presence," "we really got each other," "a playfulness in the relationship," and "Lark singing to Leslie." Lark summed up the conversation: "We saved each other's asses when we really needed each other? It was a joyous experience!"

As the first session ended, the clinical social worker asked, "What might you take away from our conversation?" Holly stated, "Remembering why we got together in the first place to save each other."

GUIDING QUESTIONS

- If working with LGBTQ+ and/or polyamorous populations are new to you, how would you ensure your own cultural competence?
- How would you begin the next session with this couple?
- Based on your theoretical background and developing practice orientation, how might you make sense of this case?
- How might you diagram their consensually nonmonogamous relationship formation? To what ends may it be helpful to include their poly family in session(s)? How might you approach that work?
- From a narrative therapy perspective, how might this case be understood? How might using the narrative therapy practices of relational interviewing, externalizing conversations, reauthoring conversations, and re-membering conversations influence the course and outcome of the clinical work? (See also references below for further background on narrative work.)

  - How might considering multistoried identities of the clients and the relationship enrich the clinical work and the outcome of the work?
  - What other models or therapeutic approaches might be helpful in unpacking the case?

CASE FORMULATION

Generalist Formulation

Lark, a forty-year-old, white trans woman (male-to-female, or MTF), and Holly, a forty-one-year-old, white, pansexual female are struggling with a change in the qualities of their eight-year marriage that have caused each of them sadness, anger, and distress. An increase in the presence of untreated anxiety, panic, and depression has emerged for each of them, as the distress in the relationship has increased. The couple is in significant psychic pain of grief and loss and is seeking help with determining the shape the relationship can take as they move forward in life. As of late, they seem to have relied on prescribed medications, alcohol, pot, and engaging in conflictive communication to mediate their concerns and challenges. Also, the extramarital activity and communication have decentered their couplehood.

Culturally Responsive and Queer-Affirmative Formulation

Lark, a nonbinary trans woman, and Holly, a pansexual cisgender woman, are facing distress, sadness, and anger as their marriage relationship of eight years has taken on a problem-saturated or deficit story. This thin description of the relationship could be potentially captured by the contemporary practices of couple therapy informed by individualism: this perspective narrows pathways of understanding by limiting the identification of cultural and contextual influences on the relationship and, as such, can essentially lead partners to view themselves, each other, and the relationship as deficit ridden and broken.

Because identities and remembrances are profoundly political, it is important to keep in mind Lark and Holly's "relationships with work," their poly family (Collin and Jack), and the cultural context of transphobia. The influence of these relationships on the marital relationship is often missed when viewed from contemporary couple therapy practices. For example, Lark's work has captured an inordinate amount of time and emotional energy away from the relationship, leaving Holly to interpret this as Lark's lack of commitment to their marriage or a viewing of the marriage as unimportant (i.e., an individual deficit). Holly and Lark live a polyamorous lifestyle, one that is not held with value in the dominant culture of heteronormativity and monosexism (Herz & Johansson, 2015; Iantaffi & Bockting, 2011). It is important to consider the influence of this cultural context on the relationship and the individual partners, including indexing the micro- and macroaggressions Lark, Holly, and the relationship experience routinely.

TREATMENT AND ACTION PLAN

- *Narrative therapy*: Narrative therapy–informed relational interviewing (RI) is the chosen therapeutic approach for working with Lark, Holly, and the relationship (Bjoroy, Madigan, & Nylund, 2016; Hedtke & Winslade, 2016; Madigan, 1996, 2008; Madigan & Nylund, in press; White, 1988–1989, 2007; White & Epston, 1990). Developed at the Vancouver School for Narrative Therapy, RI was developed for working with conflicted couple relationships. RI is a practice that invites couples to remember and appreciate foundational ethics that have shaped the relationship, opens possibilities for action, and enhances the couple's abilities to determine what shape they wish their relationship to take (Madigan & Nylund, in press). After an assessment has been completed and the couple has been consented into a narrative approach, an overview of interventive steps is as follows:

- Invite the couple to ethical remembering of conversations (Madigan, 2008; Madigan & Nylund, in press; White, 1988–1989, 2007; White & Epston, 1990).
- Read back notes from the first session, and support experience of loss and grief (Hedtke & Winslade, 2016; Madigan & Nylund, in press).
- Therapeutic letter writing: from the therapist to the couple's relationship (Bjoroy et al., 2016; Madigan, 2011).
- Invite Lark and Holly each to write letters from the relationship's point of view to the couple to be shared at the next session (Bjoroy et al., 2016; Madigan, 2011; Madigan & Nylund, in press).
- Invite Lark and Holly to read their letters aloud to one another (Bjoroy et al., 2016; Madigan, 2011; Madigan & Nylund, in press).
- Create a community of concern to support the newly emerging ethical shape of the relationship (Madigan, 2008; Madigan & Nylund, in press; White, 1988–1989, 2007; White & Epston, 1990).
- Invite Holly and Lark to cocreate a *rite of passage* for the relationship as it moves into what Michael White (1997) has called a reincorporation (Madigan & Nylund, in press; White, 2007).

■ *Feedback-informed treatment (FIT)*: Privileging the transformative power of the therapeutic alliance, it is essential to have an accurate and valid understanding of the working relationship.

This can be achieved on a continual basis using FIT's Outcome Rating Scale (during the beginning of the session) and the Session Outcome Rating Scale (at the end of session) (Chesworth et al., 2017).

■ *Couple therapy, queerly*: While one should not assume that LGBTQ+ couples have faced certain obstacles (individually or collectively) over time, practitioners should seek clarity about the presenting problem(s) from each partner and apply an ecological framework and an affirming therapeutic alliance, always foregrounding the couple's resilience (Lev, 2015). Avoiding assumptions is essential as the issues a couple may be struggling with (e.g., communication, financial, work) may be simply those issues and may have nothing to do with either partner's sexuality or gender. The uniqueness of what defines the couple outside of heteronormative frameworks is important to understand in the early stages of intake (Heck, Flentje, & Cochran, 2013) and assessment prior to treatment or during the first few sessions. Part and parcel to this, social workers should ensure that they are consistently on the same page with the couple in understanding terms, definitions, and meanings. Therefore, embracing a couple's unique queer narratives and relationship structure while deconstructing hetero- and homonormative paradigms is essential to be an affirming social worker (Hudak & Giammattei, 2014).

It would not be atypical for therapists and practitioners seeing LGBTQ+ couples to use many common tools (e.g., ecomaps, genograms) as well as to manage typical conflictual issues and defense mechanisms (e.g., sexuality, power, scapegoating, triangulation) while tuning into the couple's unique norms, values, and meanings related to monogamy, sex, relations with biological family compared to family of choice, and so on (Bepko & Johnson, 2000). Many models and theoretical

approaches that have been found to be most effective in working with LGBTQ+ couples may include behavioral approaches (see Gurman, Lebow, & Snyder, 2015). Finally, practitioners should always use the lens of relational intersectionality to understand LGBTQ+ couples' multiple identities
(e.g., gender, race, ethnicity, sexuality, gender identity, and
beyond) as critical to understanding the unique lived experiences of couples seeking therapy (Addison & Coolhart,
2015).

■ *Clinical monitoring and evaluation*: Both Lark and Holly are experiencing mood and anxiety symptoms as of late; some of
these are also long-standing. They both are distressed by these
symptoms. Based on the assessment, there should be initial and
ongoing attention to the symptoms of mood, anxiety, and panic
attacks; based on the narrative case formulation, there needs to
be ongoing assessment of the influence of these symptoms on
the relationship. In addition, the social worker should monitor
for potential emergence of suicidality (Chesworth et al., 2017;
Tilsen & Nylund, 2010). Parallel to this, a continual assessment
of Holly's relationship with alcohol is necessary, along with an
understanding of their relationships with marijuana. This may
start with the assessment, but certainly also it can be part of
psychoeducation around substances and their influences on relationships and more generally symptoms. Finally, it may be
necessary to make a referral for psychiatric medications or
supportive services around substances. Preeminent in this is
to monitor their (potential) referral experiences to ensure
trans-competent care (see World Professional Association for
Transgender Health, 2018).

REFERENCES AND RESOURCES

Addison, S. M., & Coolhart, D. (2015). Expanding the therapy paradigm with queer couples: A relational intersectional lens. *Family Process, 54*(3), 435–453.

Bepko, C., & Johnson, T. (2000). Gay and lesbian couples in therapy: Perspectives for the contemporary family therapist. *Journal of Marital and Family Therapy, 26*(4), 409–419.

Beyond Same-Sex Marriage. (2008). Beyond same-sex marriage: A new strategic vision; Executive summary. *Studies in Gender and Sexuality, 9*(2), 161–171.

Bjoroy, A., Madigan, S., & Nylund, D. (2016). The practice of therapeutic letter writing in narrative therapy. In B. Douglas et al. (Eds.), *Handbook of counselling psychology* (4th ed., pp. 332–348). London, UK: Sage.

Chesworth, B., Filippeli, A., Nylund, D., Tilsen, J. Minami, T., & Barranti, C. (2017). Feedback-informed treatment with LGBTQ clients: Social justice and evidence-based practice. In D. S. Prescott, C. L. Maeschalck, & S. D. Miller (Eds.), *Feedback-informed treatment in clinical practice: Reaching for excellence.* Washington, DC: American Psychological Association.

Gurman, A. S., Lebow, J. L., & Snyder, D. K. (Eds.). (2015). *Clinical handbook of couple therapy.* New York, NY: Guilford Press.

Heck, N. C., Flentje, A., & Cochran, B. N. (2013). Intake interviewing with lesbian, gay, bisexual, and transgender clients: Starting from a place of affirmation. *Journal of Contemporary Psychotherapy, 43*(1), 23–32.

Hedtke, L., & Winslade, J. (2016). *The crafting of grief: Constructing aesthetic responses to loss.* New York, NY: Routledge.

Herz, M., & Johansson, T. (2015). The normativity of the concept of heteronormativity. *Journal of Homosexuality, 62*(8), 1009–1020.

Hudak, J., & Giammattei, S. V. (2014). Doing family: Decentering heteronormativity in "marriage" and "family" therapy. In T. Nelson & K. Winawer (Eds.), *Critical topics in family therapy* (pp. 105–115). New York, NY: Springer International.

Iantaffi, A., & Bockting, W. O. (2011). Views from both sides of the bridge? Gender, sexual legitimacy and transgender people's experiences of relationships. *Culture, Health & Sexuality, 13*(3), 355–370.

Lev, A. I. (2015). Resilience in lesbian and gay couples. In K. Skerrett & K. Fergus (Eds.), *Couple resilience* (pp. 45–61). Dordrecht, Netherlands: Springer.

Madigan, S. (1996). The politics of identity: Considering the socio-political and cultural context in the externalizing of internalized problem conversations. *Journal of Systemic Therapies, 15,* 47–63.

Madigan, S. (2008). Anticipating hope within conversational domains of despair. In C. Flaskas, I. McCarthy, & J. Sheehan (Eds.), *Hope and despair in narrative and family therapy: Adversity, forgiveness and reconciliation* (pp. 104–112). New York, NY: Routledge/Taylor & Francis Group.

Madigan, S. (2011). *Narrative therapy: Theory and practice.* Washington, DC: American Psychological Association.

Madigan, S., & Nylund, D. (in press). Poststructuralism in couple and family therapy. In J. Lebow, A. Chambers, & D. Breunlin (Eds.), *Encyclopedia of couple and family therapy* (Vol. 3). Chester, UK: Springer International.

Moors, A. C., Matsick, J. L., Ziegler, A., Rubin, J. D., & Conley, T. D. (2013). Stigma towards individuals engaged in consensual nonmonogamy: Robust and worthy of additional research. *Analyses of Social Issues and Public Policy, 13*(1), 52–69.

Moser, C., & Kleinplatz, P. (2006). Introduction to the state of our knowledge on SM. *Journal of Homosexuality, 50,* 1–15.

Tilsen, J., & Nylund, D. (2010). Resisting normativity: Queer musings on politics, identity, and the performance of therapy. *International Journal of Narrative Therapy and Community Work, 3,* 64–70.

White, M. (1988–1989, Summer). The externalizing of the problem and the re-authoring of lives and relationships. *Dulwich Centre Newsletter,* pp. 3–20.

White, M. (1997). Challenging the culture of consumption: Rites of passage and communities of acknowledgement. *Dulwich Centre Newsletter, 2–3,* 38–47.

White, M. (2007). *Maps of narrative practice.* New York, NY: Norton.

White, M., & Epston, D. (1990). *Narrative means to therapeutic ends.* Adelaide, Australia: Dulwich Centre Publications.

World Professional Association for Transgender Health. (2018). *Standards of care for the health of transsexual, transgender, and gender nonconforming people* (7th ed.). Retrieved from https://www.wpath.org

ACKNOWLEDGMENTS

I thank Tameca N. Harris-Jackson, Henry W. Kronner, and Terrence O. Lewis for multiple levels of revision and feedback, as well as my social work students at California State University, Sacramento, for piloting and providing feedback on this collection. Also, much gratitude exists for fellow councilors on the Council on Sexual Orientation and Gender Identities and Expressions of the Council on Social Work Education (CSWE), as well as the CSWE staff and colleagues, particularly Dr. Darla Spence Coffey, Andrea Bediako, and Kathleen Dyson. Finally, I am grateful to the contributors of this text, for being vulnerable in opening up their hearts, minds, and files per se to bear witness to the work they do. And, most importantly, I have deep gratitude to the brave Queer clients and Queer social workers bringing into existence LGBTQ+ identities and Queer lifeways.

CONTRIBUTORS

TYLER M. ARGÜELLO has been a practicing social worker for over twenty-four years, primarily around community mental health, substance use, HIV/AIDS, and LGBTQ+ communities. Currently, he is an associate professor and the graduate program director in the Division of Social Work at California State University, Sacramento. Dr. Argüello's research agenda seeks to increase the effectiveness of prevention strategies and intervention work with LGBTQ+ people by attending to HIV intergenerational stress and long-term survivorship. In addition, he maintains a small private practice, provides clinical supervision, and is a licensed independent clinical social worker, a diplomate in clinical social work, and a member of the Academy of Certified Social Workers. He has been a councilor on the Council on Social Work Education's Council on Sexual Orientation and Gender Identity and Expression, and he is an ELEVATE Fellow, a National Institute of Mental Health Scholar of Prevention Research, and a Coro Fellow in Public Affairs (San Francisco).

CHRYSTAL C. RAMIREZ BARRANTI is professor of social work in the Division of Social Work at California State University, Sacramento, where she has taught since fall 2000. Dr. Barranti teaches across the Bachelor of Social Work and Master of Social Work degree programs. Her research foci have included feedback-informed therapy, LGBTQI elders, interpersonal violence, and immigration experiences. A trained narrative therapist, Dr. Barranti was part of the foundational clinical team that launched the Gender Health Center in Sacramento, California.

With a specialization in serving the gender-variant community as well as all underserved and marginalized communities, the Gender Health Center was founded to provide mental health, advocacy, and health services, including a hormone clinic. Dr. Barranti has a small clinical practice with a focus on clinical supervision.

PAM BOWERS is an associate professor of social work at Humboldt State University, located in rural Northern California. Dr. Bowers's scholarly and creative activities include community-based participatory methods for health and social justice, research with LGBTQ2S populations, scholarship of teaching and learning, and social worker professional identity development. Her teaching areas include qualitative and Indigenous research methods, program evaluation, macro practice, and Master of Social Work project courses.

RICHARD A. BRANDON-FRIEDMAN is an assistant professor in the Indiana University School of Social Work. Dr. Brandon-Friedman's social work practice experience with youth in the child welfare system and with sexual and/or gender minority youth guides his inquiry into how psychosocial experiences such as trauma, sexual education, sexual messaging, and societal messaging about sexual and/or gender minorities affect youths' sexual identity development. Through this work, he aims to help service providers understand how to best assist youth in developing a positive sense of their sexual selfhood. In addition to his continuing clinical work, Dr. Brandon-Friedman serves as chair of the Indiana chapter of the National Association of Social Workers' Committee on Sexual Orientation and Gender Identity, as a counselor for the Council on Social Work Education's Council on Sexual Orientation and Gender Identity and Expression, as social work supervisor for the Gender Health Program at Riley Hospital for Children, and on the executive board of GenderNexus, an Indiana-based organization serving gender-diverse individuals.

LAKE DZIENGEL is an associate professor of social work and the director of graduate studies at the University of Minnesota, Duluth. Dr. Dziengel is a lifelong social work educator and practitioner, with primary research interests in sexual minorities and aging, medical social work, grief and loss including ambiguous losses, resilience, and social justice. Dr. Dziengel is the author of publications on relationship longevity factors for older same-sex couples, queer gender identity, a be/coming out model, and policy processes in securing civil protections for sexual minorities, and has coauthored chapters on topics including LGBT aging and health care, as well as feminist theory in social work practice.

TAMECA N. HARRIS-JACKSON is currently a lecturer with the University of Central Florida's School of Social Work, where she teaches and has helped to developed courses in human sexuality, cultural diversity, and international social work practice. Dr. Harris-Jackson has worked as a social work clinician, supervisor, consultant, researcher, and volunteer supporting LGBTQIA+ mental health, people living with HIV/AIDS, victims of sexual assault, and undocumented children and families. She is a former cochair of the Council on Social Work Education's Council on Sexual Orientation, Gender Identity, and Expression and is a current board member and Certified Sexuality Educator with the American Association of Sex Educators, Counselors, and Therapists. She also owns a private practice in central Florida, focusing on women's mental and sexual health, and established a nonprofit centering the empowerment of women of color.

SHANNA K. KATTARI is an assistant professor at the University of Michigan School of Social Work and core faculty at the Center for Sexuality and Health Disparities. A queer, white, Jewish, cisgender, disabled, chronically ill femme, her practice and community background is as a board-certified sexologist, certified sexuality educator, and social justice advocate. Dr. Kattari's extant research focuses on understanding how power, privilege, and oppression systematically marginalize, exclude, and discriminate against people regarding their identities/expressions through negative attitudes, policies, actions, and isolation. Her work centers on disability and ableism, as well as transgender/nonbinary identities and transphobia, using an intersectional lens. Recently, she has focused on the health disparities among trans/nonbinary communities, and has worked with the community to better understand how the lack of inclusive providers increases these disparities. She is interested in examining sexuality in marginalized communities, particularly disabled adults and LGBTQIA2S+ individuals.

HENRY W. KRONNER is an associate professor at Regis College. His current research interests relate to program evaluations and teaching effectiveness. Since his doctoral work, Dr. Kronner has worked at Aurora University and Lewis University, with a focus on teaching students to be effective and competent social workers. He does this through instructing practice, human behavior, research/statistics, and diversity. In addition to teaching, he has a private practice where he provides psychotherapy to clients with depression, anxiety, trauma, and relationship challenges. He believes his practice makes him a better teacher and his teaching makes him a better social worker.

JOANNA LA TORRE is a cisgender, femme, queer, multiethnic Filipina social worker. She currently practices with transition-age youth who have experienced multiple oppressions and victimizations, supporting posttraumatic growth and healing. Her research and service work to understand Filipino mental/health disparities within frameworks of historical trauma and colonial mentality. She seeks to address the paucity of scholarship on Filipinos and to bring more empirical attention to the protective factors produced by the movement of decolonizing and re/indigenizing diasporic Filipinos. To that end, Joanna is a core member of the Center for Babaylan Studies, a seminal organization within this movement. Her community work engages in the embedded cultural and community-based responses to the persistent and rippling harms inflicted during colonization.

JUDITH LEITCH is an instructor with Widener University and is a social work practitioner and researcher of sexual and gender minority health and behavioral health and people living with HIV. Dr. Leitch has received several grants for her work, which focuses on behavioral factors that affect clinical practices and with members of these communities. Outcomes from her research emphasize the importance of focusing on practitioner skills in working with these communities, particularly in room for growth in social work practices with persons of trans* experience. Her research is informed by her own practice in this area, which she has worked in since 2000.

TERRENCE O. LEWIS has extensive clinical social work experience with individuals and families in community mental health settings and private practice. As a community-based researcher, he focuses on the relationships between churches and marginalized populations, especially LGBTQ and ethnic minority communities. His dissertation research investigated the phenomenon of LGBT-affirming black churches and their responses to the HIV/AIDS crisis. Building from there, Dr. Lewis's current research project is a narrative project with African American pastors who offer a LGBT-affirming ministry within African American communities. Dr. Lewis is a recipient of the 2018 Louisville Institute

Project Grant for Researchers. For more information about his current research project, see http://www.terrenceolewis.com/lgbt-affirmative-ministries-research-project.

GITA R. MEHROTRA is an assistant professor at Portland State University's School of Social Work. Prior to being in higher education, she was involved with antiviolence work for over a decade in a variety of capacities, including direct service, education/training, and program and organizational development, with a focus on Asian and Pacific Islander and LGBTQ communities. Dr. mehrotra has also been involved with queer and trans people of color community-building and has provided technical assistance and training to South Asian and API community-based organizations around the country. Her current research and teaching interests include domestic violence in minoritized communities; the identities and wellness of queer people of color; diversity, equity, and inclusion in social work education; and critical and feminist theories and methodologies for social work.

SARAH MOUNTZ is an assistant professor at the University at Albany. Her research focuses on the experiences of LGBTQ+ youth in child welfare and juvenile justice systems. Her most recent collaborative research project, *From Our Perspectives*, used a community-based participatory research framework to look at the experiences of LGBTQ+ former foster youth in Los Angeles County through qualitative interviewing and photovoice methods. Previously, Dr. Mountz's dissertation research used life history interviewing to explore the experiences of queer, transgender, and nonbinary young people in girls' juvenile justice facilities in New York State, with attention to how the intersection of gender identity, sexual orientation, age, race, and ethnicity informed their trajectories into and out of the juvenile justice system. She is particularly interested in LGBTQ+ and other youth activism and organizing. Before becoming a faculty member, Dr. Mountz practiced in the child welfare system for several years.

STEPH NG PING CHEUNG identifies as a multiracial, butch-adjacent, queer woman and has worked in the field of antiviolence supporting survivors across a variety of contexts for the past nine years. Steph's interests include supporting and lifting up culturally specific programming, reducing barriers to accessing resources for targeted survivor communities, and identity-based practice. Steph values radical community-based coalition work and is invested in critical dialogue and transformational care.

MEG PANICHELLI is an assistant professor in the Undergraduate Social Work Department at West Chester University of Pennsylvania. Dr. Panichelli's academic foundation in women's and gender studies instilled in her a commitment to intersectional feminist politics, antioppressive social work practice, and the values of transformative justice. In the past, she managed a harm reduction program for injection drug users and people working in the sex trades, coordinated an LGBTQ+ domestic violence program, and trained advocacy staff at a domestic violence shelter. As an Italian Irish, U.S. citizen, cis, queer, femme, Dr. Panichelli grounds her teaching and research in feminist approaches to social work, namely those that incorporate anticarceral, queer, and intersectional theories of oppression. Her research and teaching dreams include projects and courses focused on the intersections of drug use, sex trade, and pregnancy, as well as fat liberation and the criminalization of sexuality.

INDEX

CPSIA information can be obtained
at www.ICGtesting.com
Printed in the USA
LVHW111043120220
646686LV00001B/3